POLITICS OF RANDOM SELECTION

MAKING GOOD
USE OF SORTITION

Gil Delannoi

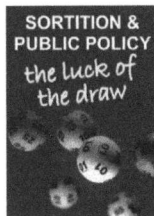

ia

imprint-academic.com

Published in the UK by
Imprint Academic Ltd., PO Box 200, Exeter EX5 5YX, UK

ISBN 9781788361255 paperback

A CIP catalogue record for this book is available from the
British Library and US Library of Congress

Contents

Preface to the English Edition

Writing an English version of *Le Tirage au sort* began rather unintentionally. I did it little by little, sometimes for a lecture, a conference or a written exchange. The result is a parallel text following the order and content of the chapters of the book published in French in 2019, but it is not a word for word, sentence for sentence translation.

The literature on sortition is made of three main genres: monographs, arguments for and against, history of the procedure in one or more dimensions. This book stands a little apart from this framework. Its method is largely deductive and theoretical in reasoning. It has a practical purpose which is aimed at specialists as well as simple users and interested parties: precise enough to satisfy an informed public and simple to be accessible to citizens and practitioners.

In the years to come, there will be much work on the table on procedural details, whatever they may be, from the referendum to random selection and other devices. It matters more than the argumentation. Before any experiment we need to know what sortition can do and already does in some cases, and what it cannot do. Properly operated, sortition can constitute another type of democracy, a democratic device of the third type which combines with the direct and the representative.

The book begins with a new typology of political regimes and institutions in contemporary societies. Its main originality is to go from the greatest generality to the detail of practices. These are as important as the principles: no procedure has a nature or essence, only uses. Tendency laws exist. They are linked to the operation (vote, draw, market, etc.) and allow many exceptions.

The book emphasizes the importance of the matrix of all the details and parameters to be settled before using the drawing of lots in various situations, for various purposes.

Academics are quicker to advise sortition to others than to apply it in the different strata and instances of universities. A special set of suggestions is offered to them in the final chapter.

Foreword

Representative democracy does not work as it should. Post-democracy is already there or visible on the horizon. This diagnosis has been made over the past few decades. There are generally two explanations. Political regimes no longer function as political bodies. Democracies are run like businesses by rulers pretending to act politically when they don't. Economic strategies and individual plans prevail. What procedures could mitigate this political flaw? These procedures are many. We will examine one of them.

The second explanation identifies rampant democratic fatigue. Partisan affiliation, or electoral loyalty to political parties, which are indispensable in a representative democracy, is in constant decline. Party systems are unstable. Nowadays abstention and electoral volatility are almost a permanent feature of elections.

Here again, a renewal of procedures could help bridging the gap. And there is no reason to be pessimistic about participation. In terms of abstention, the trend was confirmed by the French local elections of 2020, but it is contradicted by the elections in the United States in November 2020. When an issue seems very significant, people vote even during a pandemic. We must therefore consider abstention as a notable fact, but not as a definitive sign of the decline of our political systems, or as a refusal to be consulted and to participate. It is indeed important that democracy offers real options of government rather than an appearance of choice. We postulate here that a higher level of participation is good in itself. And voting is not the only way to enhance participation. Other procedures are available.

Participation cannot be limited to passive consumption of information and the exchange of comments online. Another cause of instability is the information travelling at the speed of light on social networks. Such a scattered communication fragments public debates, creating conformism bubbles rather than space for discussion. Opinions coagulate quickly but interact little. Politics is reduced to a theatre of gesticulations. Political posturing hampers long-term concerns. Distrust, frustration, suspicion are not conducive to the proper functioning of a democracy.

This weakening also stems from the economy's grip on politics. The growth rate has become the unsurpassable horizon for political decision. If markets are the sole judge of a country's politics, the political room for manoeuvre is shrinking everywhere. Many people no longer feel they're being represented and even feel betrayed by representatives prone to conformism and indifference.

By early 2020 in France no one knows what the long-term impact of the recent Yellow Jackets movement, which started in November 2018, will be. This revolt showed great hostility to the policies of the Philippe government and the leadership of President Macron. What is striking is how the debate about representation has moved out of the domain of parliamentary politics towards a questioning of the idea itself. No leader was accepted by the crowd of the movement. The Yellow Jackets do refuse to designate representatives within them. All things considered, the Brexit vote was also taken against the majority of the British parliament, the party system and representative bodies in the United Kingdom. No leader was propelled by the voters in the aftermath of the referendum.

It is true that representative democracy was not supposed to offer what it never wanted to give. The founders of representative democracies very consciously rejected popular government. They were looking to establish new political elites. In this new context, political parties asserted themselves as an interface between the public and representatives and ensured continuity between opinions and decisions. This age lasted only from the 1950s to the 1980s. It is not surprising that democracy passes periodically from one age to another. Democracy is as much a question as a solution. Conflict and instability must be transformed into democratic dynamics. The exercise must be repeated indefinitely.

What would be the contribution of better knowledge and the better practice of procedures? Is it possible to improve existing democracy without risking liquidating it? Every regime has procedures. The history of democracy shows that the use of the vote and the drawing of lots to select political office holders are basically democratic, with some precautions in the use of these instruments. Representative democracy focused on voting. The current crisis invites us to remember or discover that sortition or the use of random selection favours another type of representation which can be combined with a party system. Such a method satisfies the principles of equality, participation, impartiality, serenity. Serenity here means tranquillity of the political mind in a person and the society as well.

This book will give full place to the drawing of lots among the procedures of politics, to show its qualities and its limits, its possibilities and its constraints, its effects and its uses. It's about knowing how to use it and, first of all, knowing that there are many uses.

In Greco-Roman Antiquity the draw was deemed the procedure characteristic of any democracy. The drawing of lots was considered essential to all democratic regimes. Although its proportions and degree of use varied greatly, sortition was part of the ordinary life of democracies. It was also practised in certain aristocratic or oligarchic republics on a more restricted basis.

Two thousand years after Athenian democracy, sortition remained in some modern European republics such as Venice and Florence. From Aristotle to Montesquieu, the concept and practice of drawing lots as a defining element of democracy has survived as one of the key words in the corpus of canonical works of political theory. Montesquieu distinguished two forms of republic, the aristocratic and the democratic, both making use of sortition. The watershed moment came at the end of the eighteenth century, when the invention of a modern, extensible and effective democracy was done without the use of random selection, in practice as in theory. The lottery ceased to be understood as a republican and democratic necessity.

The creation of a modern democracy against royal absolutism also corresponds to a metamorphosis of the idea of democracy. By relying on the representation of the people rather than on their participation, the new kind of democracy abandons the practices, popular or aristocratic, which had maintained the use of sortition until that time.

The old monarchical regimes gave way to a new body politic. This politic body (or nation) votes for elites who represent them in a parliament. The idea of governing 'by the people' is detached from the principle of collective decision-making and execution. Meeting in a parliament, these representatives have to deliberate in order to reconcile two types of interests, the particular interests of their constituents and the general interest of the country.

At the beginning this new system was primarily a census system. Paying taxes gives the right to vote. The abolition of the master–servant relationship resulted in a concept of independence which removed servants and the poorest from the right to vote. At the time, making this new indirect regime more democratic, with a certain logic, consisted in amplifying popular representation by increasing its base in the election of representatives. Democratic progress tended to the adoption of universal suffrage. Voting becomes the symbol of democracy, the main modern political procedure, and finally almost the only one, so much so that the word 'vote' ends up capturing that of 'election'. The latter, however, means that a choice is made and not that it is the result of a vote.

This democratic renewal succeeded in extending parliamentary representation to the popular base. Limited suffrage was replaced by universal male suffrage in 1848 in France, then by full universal suffrage, without distinction of sex, in the 1890s and 1910s, in New Zealand, Australia and Finland, all of them forerunners but not exactly sovereign states. In the twentieth century, the political use of lotteries remained only known to historians.

A century later, since the 1990s, we are witnessing a return to sortition, remarkable in theory, shy in practice. Some pioneering works put the procedure back on the agenda. In 1989, in *Democracy and its Critics*, Robert Dahl suggested supplementing the bicameral system of the United States Congress with a third consultative chamber drawn by lot.[1] Nowadays some experiences of deliberative or participatory democracy revert to sortition after two centuries of silence.

In France, sortition as a procedure has been mentioned on the political scene by several candidates for the 2017 presidential election. These proposals are one of the many singularities of this 2017 election. They are unprecedented at this national level anywhere else. During the primary, Arnaud Montebourg proposed that a senator be chosen by lot from the citizens of each French 'département'. In a speech in Frangy he imagined a Senate designated in three thirds: a third of citizens chosen by lot, a third of scientists and technicians, and a third of elected representatives according to the procedure in force, in order to maintain a representation of the territories. Arnaud Montebourg tested the practice of drawing locally when he entrusted the task of supervising a budget and local tax increases to a jury of randomly selected citizens.

1 Robert Dahl, *Democracy and its Critics*, New Haven, Yale University Press, 1989; Barbara Goodwin, *Justice by Lottery*, Exeter, Imprint Academic, 2005 [2nd ed.]; Lyn Carson and Brian Martin, *Random Selection in Politics*, Santa Barbara, Praeger, 1999.

La France Insoumise in this election had a project which was not intended to be regular or repeated, since it suggested the draw as a procedure among others to appoint the Constituent Assembly for a Sixth Republic. This complicated device amounts to leaving the choice of procedure to the electorate. The voter is able either to vote for a representative, or to give his vote to a drawing of lots which will be carried out afterwards, in a sort of trade-off between vote and draw.

During this presidential campaign, Emmanuel Macron, on several occasions, mentioned a future organization of meetings between the President of the Republic and citizens chosen by lot. According to this proposal, each year the president has to make an assessment before an assembly or a commission of randomly selected citizens. The exercise would be prepared by the 'Cour des Comptes' (Public Court of Auditors) and would be followed by a discussion. Events have pushed him in a different direction. After the revolt of the Yellow Jackets, President Macron spent several months in a 'Great Debate' of open discussion with different groups, some participants being drawn by lot. In addition to these meetings with the Head of State, other discussion groups also used a random selection of citizens.

At the request of President, two French governments organized Citizens' Conventions (*Conventions Citoyennes*). The 150 members of this Citizens' Climate Assembly were chosen randomly by sortition. The high proportion of quota sampling in this procedure makes for a hybrid closer to stratified sampling than to a democratic lottery. The Convention was slightly delayed by the COVID pandemic and lasted from 2019 to 2020. Around 15% of its proposals were adopted by Parliament. Contrary to certain announcements, the conclusions of the Convention were not submitted to a referendum.

Another Convention of the same type (185 citizens) was convened in 2022 and 2023. Its subject was 'end-of-life support', a programme whose main issues concerned palliative care and euthanasia. Macron announced that a bill on the issue of 'end-of-life support' would be drafted before the end of the summer of 2024.

.

Introduction

To get to the heart of the matter, what can the draw be used for in general? What can be chosen by drawing lots? The draw applies to people, objects or decisions.

To individuals: sortition selects one or more from among a group. In comparison, a vote elects by counting the votes cast on each person.

To objects: sortition selects an object (sometimes from among several objects) and assigns it to one person (or more) from among a group or population. In comparison, a vote relates simultaneously to a choice of objects or individuals from among candidates (even sometimes from among a group in which everybody is considered eligible, without the existence of candidacies).

To decisions: sortition picks a decision from among several defined options. By contrast, the decision is made by vote in any group of voters, of any size and of any function. In politics, decisions are mainly taken by vote in a parliament or in a referendum.

The frequency of these various uses has not been equal in history. Sortition was sometimes used to designate people, sometimes to assign objects. It was only very rarely, almost never, used to make decisions. The ratification of a treaty or a constitutional amendment, or decisions within an organization or an institution, is not done by lot. Sometimes a decision is taken by lottery in the event of a tie in a succession of votes. This rare exception confirms the weirdness of the draw for decision-making.

One can use the draw for selecting people, things or decisions, but why and how? When this question is asked without preamble to people of all ages, of all professions, it attracts the same answer: the draw is used for games of chance and in the rules of sports competitions – the jackpot for the lotto and the draw for the teams in each phase of a football cup or another team game. The draw is therefore associated with lottery, raffle, money, sport, but very little with politics and almost never with administration.

The presence of sortition in the programmes of several presidential candidates in 2017 remains, however, anecdotal. It is the possibility of sortition which is more and more mentioned, defended, discussed, but the procedure is very rarely tried. These signs nevertheless indicate that the extension of sortition beyond a purely playful use has become plausible. This is why this book's orientation, as practical as theoretical, is looking to the future and the potential of a procedure. Only some mentions of its past will be made succinctly.

What should you do when you have decided to use the draw in a procedure? What practical questions arise? What options are available? What will be the details? What advantages and disadvantages should we expect from each option? What are the risks to know and the precautions to take?

Exploring most of the thinkable options reveals the potential of procedures. The purposes are multiple, diverse and sometimes contradictory. How to combine these options in accordance with some finality? Concrete examples give an idea of the comparative advantages, of the practical difficulties. What is there in common to conscription by lottery, the result of a raffle, a sample survey by random selection, the appointment of randomly selected officials and judges in ancient Athens, a calculation of probability, the toss at the start of a match? They have only one operation in common, which consists of subtracting from a pool or a base. Almost everything else differs. Each example teaches about the potential of sortition.

The drawing of conscripts for military service, as it was practised in France, lost its egalitarian character. Established in France during the Revolution, conscription was regulated by various forms of drawing lots from 1804 until 1905. In this process, sortition turned into trade because the number drawn could be sold. All the elected soldiers of the draw did not do the service for which they had been chosen by lot. The "winning" ticket could be transmitted, against payment, to a substitute. In fact, numbers were drawn rather than people, and those numbers were marketed afterwards. One procedure can turn more or less intentionally into another. One operation can hide another. Every point mentioned or forgotten in a regulation counts.

The practical details condition the consistency, efficiency and impact of a procedure, which depends to a much lesser extent on the material and the concrete means of the operation. A procedure is not a general idea but a set of practices. The relevance of these practices can only be measured during the procedure and according to its objective.

What matters above all is not the principle (vote, sortition, auction, test), it is not the "what" (to draw or not to draw), it is the "how" and the "why". All the effects, from mathematical to political, from sociological to psychological, expected or unsuspected, all are the results of the definition and arrangement of details. They must be examined in the observable consequences of a procedural device.

It is vital to avoid any clumsy and counterproductive use of sortition. Its most fervent supporters must understand that clumsy use would do considerable harm to the reception of the procedure they want to see applied. Any procedure includes one or more material operations. It is an ordered and coordinated sequence. It cannot be reduced to operations, but it cannot be intelligible and coherent without a firm mastery of the instruments. The following glossary specifies the use of some essential concepts.

1. **Population:** Any use of the random selection of individuals, in the political field or in another one, presupposes the existence of a population. This population is made up of all the people potentially concerned, capable of performing the future task, as citizens or inhabitants (of a state, of a country, of a region, of a city) or even as members or agents of an organization or institution.

   Examples: France, Britain or the city of Marseille, or Turin, or the wine-growing profession (legally registered), or mathematics teachers in secondary education, or such and such a company, or such and such a university.

2. **Base or Pool (of the draw):** This database is the part of a population legally retained for the draw. It lists all the qualified people (the pool) from a population to participate in the operation. The image of the pyramid makes it possible to visualize this: the top of the pyramid is the result of the draw. This base or pool can be equivalent to the population when the entire population after legal verification is listed in the database. By contrast, a restricted base is limited to a small number of people from among whom the draw is made. This restriction takes various proportions: depending on the criteria, of the order of 90, 50, 10 or 1% of a population, or even a few individuals, two being the bare minimum for any random selection. A base will therefore be equal to or smaller than the population.

   Examples: for a jury at the tribunal, only adults are retained. Among the members of a profession, if a few years of experience are required, only those with a certain number of years of experience list in the database. Likewise, if all the students of a university are chosen by lot for internal functions, the first-year students may have to wait one year or one semester before being included in the pool because they have to become familiar with the institution. A draw for military service is obviously limited by a criterion of age and physical capacity.

3. **Qualification:** Any definition of a database goes through a qualification procedure. The qualification gives the criterion defining a legal base of people taking part in any lottery draw. There are countless usable criteria, ranging from the simple verification of a population to the skill test.
Examples: in a national population only residents may be qualified, whereas non-residents are not, because they are too far away or too little concerned. The criterion is nationality. In some cases, the draw may be open to non-national residents, the criterion being residence. In other cases, the draw may concern all nationals, even non-residents. The criteria can be age: above 18, 30 or 40 years old. Another case: if the skill required by the function to be performed is precise, technical, it is necessary to be qualified on a prior test and pass it to be included in the database (or pool). Skills are very diverse. The ability of those listed in the base may be related to the writing or mastery of a language or to the knowledge of the elements essential for future functions, which may be more or less technical, more or less easy to exercise. Every qualification has to be adapted to each situation.

4. **Application (or candidacy):** It designates the act of voluntary registration in a database. The application may or may not be subject to qualification filling. This act takes place before the application form if conditions are required, or after the acceptance of the application form if a test is necessary to qualify the candidates for the draw.

5. **Refusal (to be registered in a base):** This is the possibility that a candidate might not appear in the base, or might withdraw from it before the draw, either by expressing a refusal prior to any possibility of registration (strong refusal, comparable to abstention), or by asking to be withdrawn from a registration already made by an administration, which can then be done piecemeal or for short or long durations.

6. **Withdrawal:** This designates the right to resign from one's election after the draw, after the transaction (*ex post*). This

withdrawal occurs after the drawing operation and before the appointment for the function. The selected person, by withdrawing, frees a place for a person who has arrived further down on the list of people chosen by lot.

7. **Selection by lot:** The person chosen by lot is a person selected by the drawing operation. To study the stages of the procedure, the parallel with voting is essential.

Draw → elements drawn → (s) election = having been chosen by lot.

Vote → ballot → (s) election = having been chosen by vote (habitually: elected).

The possibility of using the word election may surprise when it comes to the draw. It is, however, entirely appropriate, if only by comparison with a vote. Both procedures require a population, a base and then an election operation. What is the difference? Voting proceeds by adding votes on names (or options) whereas drawing is by extraction of names (or numbers). In both cases, the final designation of those elected constitutes the result of the election. Regardless of the operation to be carried out, it does not matter whether this election is the result of an addition of votes or a subtraction of one or more names from among a pool or population. At the end of the process, there are people who are elected or people to whom objects are assigned. And vote indeed can also be used for assigning objects or items to individuals or groups. That said, if the word "elections" is a source of possible confusion among the public, the word selection is just as good and "chosen by lot" becomes the usual expression.

8. **List:** This word refers to the extensive nomination of all the people included in a database before the draw (as preparation) and to the final list of the persons chosen by lot (result). There are therefore several lists to be considered in a draw: a listed population, a listed qualified legal base, that of the persons chosen by lot, each going down in size. This last list, if it is ordained (drawn first, second, etc.), constitutes a reserve

making it possible to supplement, if necessary. This reserve serves to replace people in the event of withdrawal after the draw or resignation during the term of office. This list of selected officials (kept secret or published) avoids carrying out a new and partial drawing operation each time a replacement is required.

***

To begin with, we must describe an operation, its mechanism, its devices. An operation is a concrete action following a method. It evokes calculation. Like a vote, the draw is a calculation. One or more individuals, elements or objects are extracted from a set, a pool or a database. All lottery draws subtract from a base. As a metaphor, it is not so different from an operation in the surgical sense, which often involves extraction by manipulation. This is an extraction from the body politic to become part of a smaller internal and specialized body. It is therefore a temporal extraction, a sort of internal and momentary graft, with a return to the usual place in the body politic. The metaphor has its limits.

What exactly does subtract mean? Consider removing apples from a basket at random, without first examining them. How many to take and how to get them out of the basket? The draw, as an operation, is this gesture of subtracting one or more apples, blindly, without observing before taking one or the other. Many? Sometimes all of them. If it is all of them, the subtraction exhausts the base by going to the end of the possible draw. It amounts to registering an order of appearance of objects which, in the end, were all removed from the database. This is a specific, exhaustive draw, in order to obtain a classification by successive subtraction of individuals.

Any drawing operation is between two limits: drawing a single one or drawing all the elements. The operation subtracts an item, some or all. The latter case is only of interest if the order of appearance is taken into account. Otherwise, it would suffice to switch the contents of the basket to another. Apart from border-line cases, the drawing operation subtracts one or more elements and leaves a remainder. Though this remaining part may sometimes be smaller than the number of selected elements, in most cases it is larger or very much larger than the selected part of the base.

The operation can be direct or indirect. It's direct when I draw apples to get them. It is indirect when I subtract items that represent people or other objects which cannot be physically captured. People are not put in a big bag from where they are removed with large pliers. The draw is made using material supports: cards, tokens, tickets, numbers, which represent people, goods, options, objects of the draw. Between the direct operation (subtracting things directly from the base) and the indirect operation (subtracting a symbol), there are intermediate cases, for example if I have the choice to open one door among five knowing that one person is behind each door.

A draw as a method links the operation itself to the procedure which frames and explains it. The draw only makes sense through the procedure which includes the operation. Only the procedure as a whole allows us to understand what the operation is made for.

A procedure is a non-random sequence of operations. The operations which form the procedure are only practised and can only be practised in a certain order. Consider the increasing number of procedures that a computer installer or the software itself must perform. Steps in a procedure cannot be changed or reversed without causing the entire process to fail.

In the legal sense, the procedure is the methodical process which guarantees the respect of the letter of an act, a law or a regulation. Any anomaly or fraud removes all or part of its legality. To respect the procedure, in this sense, it is first of all necessary to avoid fraud or errors, to be attentive to the detail of the operations, in order to obtain a rigorous and incontestable result. A cooking recipe is the most ordinary and familiar procedure in the world. Here, too, the operations must follow one another in the correct order. In case of error or negligence, the result is certainly not illegal, except fraud or poisoning, but it is inedible, indigestible, unpleasant or, at the very least, tasteless.

In the drawing of lots, the elements of the base are often identified by a number or by a name. In addition, the choice of process, instrument or mechanism, which accomplishes the subtraction of one or more elements in a base, is almost infinite. It suffices to carry out the subtraction. The most common instruments in a draw are the coin for a binary choice (heads or tails), the dice for a multiple choice (usually six or twelve options), the balls (numbered or containing a ticket), tickets, cards, tokens. Natural elements (blades of grass, petals, shells, stones) were used in traditional societies.

More complex and faster machines are used when the draw requires many repeated operations, for example, to pull several hundred items from among several thousand or millions. The Athenian *kleroterion* was a machine for inserting and removing tokens. The apparatus quickly selected the numerous citizens sworn in the copious juries of the Athenian Popular Tribunal: juries of 501, 1,001, 1,501 people.

It is possible, without equipment but with method, to draw on the basis of the occurrence of events: number of birds in a flight, figures given spontaneously by a person ignoring the items or individuals previously attached to these figures. In summary, any device making it possible to carry out subtraction by drawing is suitable. If I attached an option to each vowel in the alphabet, I just need to open a random book and select the first vowel from the first line to draw one of the options. There is no shortage of methods as long as the subtraction tool is well designed. In this sense, drawing lots is a materially easy operation. The use of coins or dice is particularly conducive to mathematical reasoning, probability theory and combinations. In political and social use, numbered or nominative tickets or tokens are the most common instrument.

By clarifying the essential words, acts and concepts, we have distinguished operation from procedure. We can now consider the multiple uses of the lottery, their respective advantages and disadvantages, the arguments for and against the choice of such a procedure. First, the drawing of lots will be characterized among all comparable procedures. Since we spontaneously oppose the drawing of lots to the vote or to the test (examination), as other means of selection among people or objects, the drawing of lots must be studied within the framework of a typology of the very few fundamental procedures. They are not many. This little procedural theory necessarily opens a perspective on all political regimes.

Chapter 1

Procedures and Political Regimes

How can we select a person or several ones in a group in order to perform a task of general interest, requiring neither learning nor specialization? What methods are available?

Suppose that only one person is to be designated. Only one volunteer comes forward. Supply equals demand. Yet this volunteer can be tacitly accepted by the group or not. What if several volunteers come forward? Volunteering became a candidacy and candidates appeared. A choice remains to be made. And what if there is no volunteer? Volunteering is a minimal method. It is hardly formalized. It is often below the procedural level. Volunteering is necessarily involved in certain procedures but is no procedure in itself. A set of options is available to go beyond volunteering or to make up for the lack of volunteers. A formalized method becomes a procedure.

Six Options, Six Procedures

1. Voting to elect on the basis of candidacies is an option. The volunteers are therefore in the position of candidates. It is also possible to consider that everyone is eligible. The vote can be cast for anyone belonging to the group. Election without a candidate, although less frequent, is possible when all are

considered as candidates by nature, or eligible even against their will, which amounts to the same thing.

2. Another option is to do a test to find the most capable of performing the task. In this exercise, it was established that all people had approximately the required capacities. A test is necessary when the task requires technical skills, but useless when the task requires no particular capacity.

3. Another option is to adopt as a criterion a biological or physical marker: the oldest or the youngest, the largest or the smallest, the heaviest or the lightest. In this way, by descent or by any other follow-up, someone could, over a longer period, inherit the task. Heredity is one way of passing on the biological marker.

4. When everyone has approximately equal competence (for the task), neither applications nor tests are essential. The draw is a quick and easy option. If necessary, the qualification of a base makes it possible to draw lots after having carried out the qualification which reduces the base to the competent people, the draw being associated with another procedure (classification, test, biological criterion).

5. The following option, although not very political, involves paying the person or selling the function: setting a price, perhaps at auction, in a supply and demand process. Buying and selling creates a market. You will have to pay the fee to perform an attractive or rewarding task, or you will have to be paid if it comes to a chore. The interest of the group is to pay the least or sell as high as possible. The interest of the performer is obviously the opposite. The execution of the task will be sold to the most motivated or wealthy volunteers or it will be paid to the least demanding of candidates.

6. Membership in a party or any other type of membership in an association remains an option, often close to volunteering. The difference between membership and volunteering is that membership is based on belonging and sharing. It is mostly about joining a group. The execution of a task or a function

comes next and is not mandatory. The condition for entering an association is akin to a more or less developed rite. The smallest rite is to receive proof of membership, by card or ticket. Some rites are more complicated, but rarely insurmountable if you do it with good will and perseverance.

This rather simple exercise revealed the three fundamental political regimes as defined by Aristotle. They are the source of all typologies of political regimes. Indeed, attribution according to a biological criterion (filiation, inheritance) is the procedure most familiar to the government of one, the monarchy. The vote tends to designate a qualified, popular or ambitious elite. Aristocracy, in Greek, means the power of the best. Sortition, by giving everyone an equal chance to serve as an official in different positions, produces a more egalitarian effect than the other methods. While democracy is certainly not defined only by equality, it is nonetheless the most egalitarian of regimes, barring exceptions or inconsistencies.

For Aristotle, the monarchy is most often based on inheritance and descent. Aristocracy or, in the modern sense, meritocracy is based on qualification, co-option and, for a variable part, election by a more or less popular vote. Democracy such as it was in Athens uses sortition for selecting citizens who have to execute the decisions in order to put into practice the popular vote of laws. The modern equivalent would be people chosen by lots for implementing decisions passed by referendum.

Aristotle was the first theorist who systematically studied these questions and defined their terms. He distinguishes political regimes according to several criteria: the number of holders of sovereign executive power; the main and most characteristic procedure of the political system; the archetype of social and interpersonal relationships specific to each regime.

The ancient definition gave its name to regimes in accordance with the number of holders of supreme power. This refers to the most visible, the most spectacular: who exercises supreme power or at least appears as such an official holder—one, several or all members of the body politic. Our political vocabulary still bears this mark: monarchy means a single sovereign; aristocracy means several; democracy means all citizens in Aristotle's time, all adults of both sexes by universal suffrage now.

The definition of the regime by its typical procedure is as important as the definition of the regime by the holder of the sovereign power. Reciprocal attractions and repulsions between procedures and regimes matter much in the definition of political regime, perhaps even more than the number of sovereign rulers (one, many, all). The relationships between regime and procedure allow hybridizations. An aristocracy practising the drawing of lots will tend to democratize. A democracy in which the vote dominates the draw tends to become meritocratic and oligarchic.

Cross-Tabulation of Regimes and Procedures

Since Aristotle, other procedures have become important in political systems. It is also by these procedures that these modern systems can be identified. We saw them appear among the answers in our initial exploration of possible procedures for selecting one or few from among a group: the market, the test and the membership.

1. An association is generally based on the will to belong, to cooperate, to serve the organization. Membership, especially of political parties, is essential in a representative democracy. This right of association, based on the principle of voluntary service, is also the basis of trade union activities, non-governmental organizations, associations of all kinds, for all purposes (including recreational) and all types of clubs, large or restricted. Membership is the most common principle of religions, churches, sects and religious practice, all of which often play a considerable political role, even if they do not define a specific political regime; apart from the rather rare hypothesis of theocracy, a subtype of oligarchy or aristocracy.

2. Another essential procedure is the test (or examination) which measures a technical learning and certifies a specialization. It is essential in all bureaucracies, public and private, as well as in many commercial, craft, industrial, academic activities.
3. Finally, the market, as the interaction of offers and demands regulated by a legal procedure (in this different from barter), is binding on all commercial firms, enterprises and factories. Moreover, beyond the strictly commercial sphere, the market is an element present in the procedures as soon as the profitability of an activity, even very partially, comes into play.

Orientation for the procedure	Operations or criteria	Political regime or typical institution	Type of referendum in the classical regimes or main institution in the modern types
Heredity	Filiation Option	Monarchy	Plebiscite
Vote	Representation Mandate	Aristocracy Oligarchy	Infrequent referendums
Lottery	Qualification Drawing of lots	Democracy	Frequent referendums
Supply and Demand	Auction Price	Market	Company Business Propriety
Technical Competence	Test Competition	Bureaucracy Meritocracy	Agency Department Ministry
Membership	Volunteering Admission	Association	Party Trade Union Church, Sect Club

Table 1. Cross table of regimes and procedures.

A. The columns indicate procedures, operations, regimes.
Examples: the second column compares the operations characteristic of the regimes. Today, we inherit by descent or by being designated by will. However, other methods of appointment are possible: one can represent someone else by exercising a mandate; one is qualified for a draw and then

drawn from a base; a position is purchased by auction or other fixation procedure; a test certifies after a competition or another kind of assessment the ability to take up employment. Membership allows volunteers to be linked within an association. In the latter case, none of the previous operations was necessary: neither birth, nor vote or draw, nor right of access by purchase or by test. Admission is consecutive to volunteering and the access conditions are, in general, not very restrictive. As a procedure, admission to an association is not exempt from rite, but it is distinguished from the more constrained and limited operations specific to other procedures and regimes. This does not mean that one is always admitted to an association or that being excluded from it is impossible. There are very closed clubs which, in fact, resemble elective oligarchies. Their high degree of closure confirms, by exception, that the militant and proselytizing tendency of mass associations (parties, churches, movements) is based on a large voluntary service, moreover much more often passive than a candidacy or a test.

B. The rows aggregate the basic elements of a political regime or a type of organization.

Examples: the monarchy is often hereditary and sometimes elective. Even as general procedure without political meaning, inheritance, when it is not imposed by filiation, is transformed into an inheritance attributed solitarily, discreetly and therefore in an almost monarchical manner by the person who transmits the inheritance. His choice is sovereign.

We find the typology of Aristotle in the three usual regimes passed in the political vocabulary (and for the first three rows). This typology must be extended to the three other types of organization (market, bureaucracy, association) essential in an industrial society. On one hand, it is impossible to think and practise politics today without bureaucracies, markets and associations. These three quasi-regimes are so powerful that they sometimes come to dominate the three others. On the other hand, from the point of view of the supreme power, as regards their direction or mode of government, these three types are not completely separated from to the three other perspectives. An association can have a management of monarchical, aristocratic or democratic type.

These types are obvious but only tendential. There are mixed types, combined. Not all aristocracy is elective. Any election by vote is not aristocratic. But every election by vote tends to create an elected elite. At the same time, the elites tend to legitimize and maintain themselves through restricted or popular, regular or fraudulent votes. Likewise, tendentially, whatever its size, from a small committee to a population, a lottery often evens and democratizes at the level at which it is carried out.

All the prevailing links (monarchy-heredity, aristocracy-election, market-auction, etc.) reflect a dominant tendency in society or in one of its spheres. However, any strong tendency admits secondary combinations: elective monarchies, hereditary aristocracies, ancient democracies without sortition, modern non-democratic drawing of lots (raffles, lotteries).

A modern state is a bureaucracy, it subcontracts with companies (market), applies legislation drafted by elected officials and assemblies elected by vote (often by universal suffrage), influenced by associations (parties, unions, lobbies, various groups). It admits inheritance between members of a family or between individuals. Its courts include magistrates recruited by bureaucratic procedures and juries of citizens chosen by lot.

Vast and multiple, this combination is not, however, total. Some possible combinations are non-existent, some intersections remain empty. A monarchy by lot? An hereditary bureaucracy?

Procedures rarely disappear. Example: inheritance remains the basis for the individual transmission of property. In contemporary politics, heredity is in decline: few political regimes are absolute monarchies. In some unexpected situations, it subsists *de facto* if not *de jure*. Communist regimes have created monarchical habits unexpected by their designers: a dynasty settles in North Korea, Fidel Castro is replaced by his brother in Cuba. The Soviet and Chinese regimes are bureaucratic oligarchies. We even see this in democracies: with the Bush and Clinton families in the United States, for example. The unofficial, sometimes half-hidden practice of procedures is readable as the tinkering of regimes, as effective as the official combinations of the ruling strata.

The Aristotelian reasoning goes back and forth between the definition of regimes and the choice of procedures. It included a double meaning "cause → effect → cause"; for example, "monarchy → heredity → monarchy". In other words, the monarchy tends to accentuate and multiply hereditary procedures (monarchy → heredity). But, circularly, the other way round, in an opposite direction, a hereditary procedure tends to make any type of regime monarchical (heredity → monarchy).

These circular relationships remain. Only the "democracy → lottery → democracy" relationship has almost disappeared. Although it was essential in the differentiation of regimes, sortition is now seen as a poor and obsolete procedure. It is found very little as such, very little even as a hybridized marginal procedure with the other five procedures. When it comes to defining democracy, can we nevertheless consider it to be a type in its own right?

Chapter 2

A Third Type of Democracy

Different types of democracy have existed in theory and in practice, first and foremost: ancient and modern, popular or representative. Our democratic past was built at two decisive historical moments. No theory is possible without referring to these two sources.

Genesis of Democracy

The first and, in some measure, the sole type of democracy mainly based on sortition developed in ancient Greece, especially in Athens. The old democratic city-state system was based above all on a popular assembly, a meeting place where all citizens were called several times a year to take the most important decisions. This popular assembly (*ekklesia*) voted the laws and political and strategic orientations by popular votes, bringing together several thousand voters. It thus constitutes a localized form of direct democracy, combining the principle of the assembly (deliberation) and the principle of the referendum (voting of decisions by all). The People's Assembly elected a board of ten *strategoi*, equivalent to our ministers and generals.

It is now forgotten, misunderstood or neglected that the most original and central principle of this democracy was the obligation of citizens to execute the decisions themselves. They had to carry out in person the decisions they had made in the assembly. It was required to pay with one's person, to contribute concretely to the functioning of the political system in every branch: legislative, judiciary and executive. The duty to perform complemented the right to decide. Concrete participation was therefore required for most executive and judicial tasks. Such an operation was only made possible by the intensive use of the lottery. Those selected ran the risk of having to implement the decision. Voting for war meant that you were likely to go fighting on the battle ground. Even in less dramatic occasions, this principle applied. Such a system entails some sense of realism and responsibility in every citizen.

Several times in his life, an Athenian citizen was chosen by lot to sit on the Tribunal in a popular jury. This office was the most frequently exercised by a citizen. The draw could also designate him as a member of the Council of 500, the body responsible for ensuring the functioning of the political system. Socrates, as a member of the Council of 500, happened to have chaired the Council and the People's Assembly. Most citizens served for various collegial executive functions, civil, public and military tasks, tasks which are now performed by the police, army or administration.

This system of intensive democratic participation declined after Alexander's conquest of Athens and became residual when Greece was transformed into a Roman province. The institutions survived only within the municipal framework. The use of lottery no longer mattered much in theory or in practice. Yet, carried by its brilliant past, Athens retained an intellectual and artistic role in the ancient world. Its example continued to fascinate procedural historians and advocates of sortition.

Athens was the centre of political philosophy. It is the birthplace of the vocabulary and typologies of our political lexicon. Politics, democracy, oligarchy, monarchy are Greek words. Plato and Aristotle, by analysing and discussing the role of the lottery, inscribed it forever in the corpus of political philosophy.

It is hardly conceivable or plausible to reinstate an Athenian system as such, in particular its extensive use of lottery and its absence of professional administration. Cornelius Castoriadis, admirer of Athens, is correct in concluding that it would be futile to attempt to reproduce the ancient experience out of context. But he judges with as much reason that it is essential to know precisely this ancient experience and to draw inspiration from it.

Restoring an Athenian-type system would be a programme of utopian magnitude, even at the level of a large city. Such a project would require all adults to devote about 20 days a year to deliberating and voting in a popular assembly. To this should be added several years entirely devoted to public tasks performed by citizens chosen by lot, with an almost certain probability for everyone to serve once in a lifetime and the possibility of serving several times. Finally, these functions would be mainly executive tasks: police, guard, caregiver, gardener and other public services. Such a project seems too demanding for the people whose life consists in behaving as producers and consumers. Objections and obstructions of the educated elites are moreover very predictable: there would be no question leaving the deliberation and decision-making to each and anyone. Besides, these elites would not find it to their taste to put on the modest clothes of employees.

The impossibility of reproducing an example in no way excludes our position in relation to what we know (or think we know) about ancient democracy. References to Athenian democracy and the Roman Republic were strongly present in the minds of actors during modern revolutions, in England, France and the United States. Reference was made, but these modernizers were looking for a new synthesis and were not very attracted by a People's Democratic Republic. They devoted themselves to the abolition of a monarchical and hierarchical past. The many symbolic (Phrygian cap) and architectural (ancient colonnades) allusions were more decorative than substantial.

Appropriating and recomposing past elements is, at all times, the hallmark of political innovation. We have to assimilate, recombine, adapt, complete and modify. The divergence between ancient democracy and modern democracy does not mean that the old and the modern democracy are radically incompatible. The opposition of principles and practices only signals that their combination has limits. While it is impossible to combine all of their respective qualities, it is possible to combine some elements.

The ancient type of democracy was not carved out of a single block of ancient marble: there are great differences between the democratic regimes that Aristotle described in his political books. In some cities, the use of voting dominated the use of lottery. In others, the two procedures balanced out. Sometimes the two procedures remained a source of conflict. There were egalitarian systems in which citizens had the same rights. In other cities, the wealthy or aristocratic class retained the main prerogatives. Cities with a census-based regime left the voting of laws, the election of leaders and the conduct of affairs to a small number of aristocrats who acted under the gaze of the people. In many ways the Roman Republic was aristocratic and popular rather than democratic. Its hierarchical organization and its popular army subdued Athenian democracy.

It was common to all these ancient experiences that the citizens (all, almost all or only a part) gathered in a public place, voted the laws and elected the leaders. The use of the lottery was extensive or restricted, it was rarely absent.

Laws adopted in ancient democracies were revisable by a political body of citizens. These cities were democratic because people often had the first and last say in politics. Part of aristocratic (or meritocratic) practice has remained in the hands of an elite of speakers who dominated the debates. Elected leaders worked out political projects, conducted foreign policy, commanded the army of citizens.

The modern revolution was as much a societal change as it was a regime change. The new type of democracy was designed to put an end to the practices specific to monarchical and clerical societies based on unequal rights at birth. At this point, building a society of equals was more urgent than the participation and representation of citizens. In 1789, the Declaration of equal, collective and individual Rights precedes the new Constitution in France. This revolution is the work of representatives in a monarchical framework who do not want to abolish, but to transform and extend, the procedure of representation by which they have been elected. They transferred it to the nation. It was therefore possible to grant equality to all these new modern citizens without representing a people in an egalitarian way and even without giving them much say in politics.

Representation is a concept and a procedure inherited from the *Ancien Régime*, which practised it in aristocratic, nobiliary, clerical and corporate forms. Democratized representation is not a pure invention. This second type of democracy is characterized by the importance given to representation rather than participation. Electing representatives exempts the people from passing laws and exempts them from serving as randomly selected citizens, except for military service.

The first type of democracy strongly encourages participation. The second one, modern and indirect, hardly mobilizes the population, except in war. Policy is decided in parliament, in government, and is subject to administrative and bureaucratic implementation. These practices, already existing under the monarchy, were increasingly inevitable in an industrial society which requires infrastructure, education, administration. That nevertheless did not imply the abandonment of most elements of the first type of democracy.

The eminent and eminently symbolic place of the first type is the popular assembly passing laws in the amphitheatre, in the forum or in the main public square. The symbolic place of the second type is the parliamentary building, house or chamber where two powers meet, the executive and the legislative. This new system, which leads to competition between political programmes for a legislative mandate, results in the existence of political parties. These political associations (from giant to dwarf) develop programmes and invest the candidates. We owe this new type of democracy two practical conditions essential to any democracy worthy of the name: the existence of a legal and protected opposition, the peaceful succession of clearly distinct policies.

What idea of the first type of democracy had the modernizers who created the second? Athens was not the only example they knew. Most ancient or pre-modern democracies (in the Middle Ages, Renaissance, for example) were not as radical as the Athens of Pericles. The second type was developed by its designers and actors in order to retain the best and avoid the worst of the ancient kind of democracy. Representation is not only a procedure avoiding the direct voting of laws, it is a principle of building society into a nation of individuals equal in law. Representatives should represent the nation as a whole and not particular or partisan interests, at least in theory.

Conversely, in the old model it was not necessary to proclaim popular sovereignty which was practised day after day by popular votes in the assembly and numerous juries of citizens chosen by lot. The second type, in compensation, must make popular, national and state sovereignty all the more sacred as it makes an indirect, representative use of it, distant from citizens.

As a result, the succession of opposite political elites governs a population which is only embodied as a political people on the day of the election of representatives, on the day of the rare referendums and, in conflictual and partial form, by street demonstrations of opponents. This distance was wanted. Jean-Jacques Rousseau deplored it and Joseph Schumpeter appreciated it. On this point, the modern type was deliberately established against an ancient heritage incompatible with representation, since the latter is entrusted exclusively to the social, political, economic, academic elites.

Active or Descriptive Representation

If the drawing of lots has been almost erased by modern democracy, it has not completely disappeared from procedures. While the modern type no longer uses procedures based on random selection in the executive and legislative branches, a lottery is sometimes used for military service or for popular juries of the courts.

Today, in 2025, any existing democracy comes from the representative model. None dates from Greco-Roman Antiquity. The tradition of popular assemblies in certain Germanic Swiss cantons (Landsgemeinde) is medieval. It is not this local survival which is the basis of the original character of the Swiss Confederation regime, but the intensive use of the referendum. Switzerland is the only contemporary sovereign state to combine the participatory type and the representative type in equal parts. Its regime is less participatory than an ancient Athenian-style regime, but incomparably more participatory than any other modern regime. Citizens are sure to have the last word if a small number sign a petition against a recent law. As the Swiss example shows, the two types of democracy lend themselves to hybridizations and can be combined without difficulty. For now, however, this modern convergence doesn't include sortition.

We must avoid being trapped with words: the same words do not always have the same meaning and do not always refer to the same practice. The word "representation" and its practices fall between two poles: on one hand, the delegation of a mandate by a population to its representatives, on the other hand the constitution of a reduced model of this population. These two very different conceptions lead to very different practices. I follow Hanna Pitkin's lead on this important point.

A representation is said to be descriptive when it faithfully reflects the composition of the population represented. The procedure must then ensure that the representatives who have been chosen from among the population, by a concentrated mirror effect, in a reduced model, resemble it, keeping the same characteristics in the same proportions.

In contrast, the other form of representation is said to be active: representatives are appointed by the population to act on their behalf and in their stead. To do this, it is not necessary that such representatives resemble the people. It is often even better if they don't resemble them because they are more qualified and better prepared for acting on their behalf. For this reason, if we only know the representatives in an active representation procedure, it would not be impossible to infer the composition of the represented population. This is not a scale model. This is not a sample.

Sometimes the representative does not even belong to the population represented. In the most formal case, this results from an impossibility or a prohibition. A lawyer cannot be the equivalent of the person he is defending. He cannot be accused, and even less guilty, of the facts advanced by the prosecution and would be dismissed if he were suspected. A lawyer represents an accused as an active representative and not as a descriptive representative. The same applies when a diplomatic body from a third country takes charge, in a crisis situation, of the interests and property of another diplomatic body, expelled by the host country.

Sometimes, however, an active representative is representative in descriptive terms as well, but this rarely matters in the process. The addition of an identity or socio-economic similarity is not necessary. Communist leaders were not all proletarians. The leaders of the conservative parties are not all heirs from rich families. A lack of descriptive representativeness does not detract from the active character of the representation. Often it even makes it more effective. We can have a great interest in being represented by someone other than ourselves — very different, more competent or more learned, less involved and less passionate.

Given our types, compared to the old model, modern democracy of the indirect type is more representative, but only in the sense of active representation. It is the principle that creates its very idea and it is the practice that supports it. On the contrary, the old type, by its direct popular nature, hardly needed descriptive representation. A popular vote or a referendum removes the question of representativeness, because it mobilizes the entire political and electoral body. The accuracy of the representation is then limited only by abstention. A referendum with compulsory voting would completely describe the population.

Descriptive representation is essential for samples, surveys, polls (by random selection or by quotas). This way of representing is not, to date, the main characteristic of any present type of democracy. As we have just seen, it is superfluous in the direct type and it is avoided, for good or bad reasons, in the indirect type. In the latter, active political representation is obtained by the coalition of partisan wills and by competition between competing programmes. There follows a relentless and imperfect adjustment between what the parties are proposing and what the electorate expects. This gap is big or small, but inevitable.

Decision-making by a citizens' assembly, typical of the ancient democratic republics, is roughly comparable, *mutatis mutandis*, to a series of referendums after joint deliberation in the public square. Organizing popular meetings, debates and then votes, several dozen times a year, was staple food for political life. On this point, it would be wrong to make the slightest comparison between a popular assembly and a parliamentary assembly. The latter is elected once every four, five or six years to deliberate all or most of the year.

Could the Athenian Council (Council of 500 or Boulè) pass for an assembly? At first glance, perhaps: it was made of 500 citizens chosen by lot to be active for a year as organizers of the political regime. It functioned, however, as a deliberative, executive and administrative body, and not as a parliament. This People's Council was rather well representative in descriptive terms, but it was thanks to the lottery and with a share of basic qualification in the pool of possible members of the Council. Its role was important: control the regularity of procedures, ensure the daily functioning of the political system, prepare the votes of the popular assembly, assist the ten leaders (*strategoi*) elected by the people. These tasks do not correspond to the ordinary work of a modern parliamentary assembly. The purpose of the Council of 500 draw was to be participatory, executive, mobilizing. In these institutions, being a people's adviser was an honour, a duty, a service, sometimes a chore. It was not a position, nor a career, nor a mandate, nor the militant application of a programme, nor membership in an elite of decision-makers.

To see descriptive representation in the old type, we should look at the Popular Tribunal (Diskasterion). The modern idea of descriptive representation was really approached there. Citizen juries in courts are held without professional magistrates. These grand juries brought together several hundred citizens chosen by lot. They were the size of a modern parliamentary assembly (501) and sometimes larger (1,001, 1,501). They gave their verdict by voting after hearing the parties. First reason for such a large size: to pronounce a popular judgment in which all kinds of people, citizens, all classes and professions, were represented. Second reason: it was impossible to bribe or influence so many people designated the same day and for one procedure only. Thus the Tribunal was both descriptive and active. Descriptive in terms of the number of jurors, and active because around 3, 5 or 10% of the total number of citizens were given the task of judging as would the general population have done. The procedure was not made in the name of the people but conducted by the people. Socrates, during his trial, addresses the 501 judges as if he were speaking to the whole population.

In the juries, on the side of the moderns, we find, on the contrary, the small number. Courts use committee-sized juries. Sometimes chosen by lot, they give a verdict within the limits provided by law, to clarify and delimit a final sentence, the details of which are pronounced by professional judges. In the judicial field, sortition has been practised, but very differently, in the two types of democracy.

Random selection has the very interesting feature of being an operation suitable for both types of representation. It supplies a very representative sample, provided the sample is large enough. The most general and fundamental characteristics of a population (age, sex, class, income, habitat) are present after the draw. A draw of 1,000 people in a country like France will be representative of the proportions of the population and a sample of 10,000 will be precisely representative.

The drawing of lots allows just as much to delegate to a few people (very few, only one if necessary) a function, deliberative or executive, advisory or active. To designate a person destined to accomplish a complex task, voting or co-opting have always been preferred. Athenian leaders (*strategoi*) were elected by the popular assembly. No sort of lottery was involved in this process. Proof that their competence, even their virtuosity, was at stake above all in the exercise of their functions.

For a diametrically opposed effect, the president of the Prytanes was designated by the draw for 24 hours as the supreme representative of the city. He was the equivalent of a ceremonial head of state, possessing, in a fleeting but very real way, the seals and other attributes of the office. Thus the head of state was chosen by lot for ceremonial functions. How better to underline the anti-monarchical character of Athenian democracy?

The leaders, on the other hand, were elected by the people for the sake of efficiency in action and quality in deliberation. During his last twenty years, Pericles was, with few exceptions, constantly re-elected. This consistency is exceptional. This underlines that the most competent were allowed to serve the city permanently through election by vote. It was also necessary to be constantly accountable and face accusers. By these procedures, the Athenians had rulers who could not behave like masters.

Election by vote, as compared to the draw, lends itself much better to active representation than to descriptive representation.

Aristotle was right to emphasize the mechanically elitist aspect of electing. The effect is inevitable whether it is a one-person election or a list ballot. Candidates are few, and those elected fewer. They therefore form a small number apart and generally known to the public.

On the other hand, a vote designed to have a descriptive effect must be surrounded by exceptional procedural constraints. An example will be more telling than a long reasoning. Today, we often wonder how to achieve gender parity among elected officials, particularly among members of assemblies. A lottery would ensure this kind of parity easily and without strong constraints or complications, because such a balanced, proportionate result derives from its pure and simple application, subject to a few conditions very easy to meet, related to the composition of the base and the number of people chosen by lot.

In the current population, the number of women is slightly higher than the number of men. To postulate that these numbers are equal does not call into question the reasoning. Let there be a group (or sample, or assembly) of 100 people chosen by lot from among a much larger population—the probability of obtaining 100 women or 100 men is close to zero, since it is in total, in both cases, $\frac{1}{2}$ to the power of 100. Conversely, the most probable distributions will lie in an interval where women and men will be in equal or nearly equal number. After 100 draws, the probability of having between 40 and 60 women or men is 96%. The law of large numbers gives a probability of having 50% (perfect parity) slightly higher than 49–51, itself higher than 48–52, etc. By repeating a random experiment, we approach a threshold value of about 50–50%.

In short, parity, or quasi-parity, is ensured by the operation of the draw without any constraints or complications. In contrast, a vote must be extremely constrained and complicated to achieve a comparable result.

The most common process used to achieve parity so far is to force parties to propose a turn to a person of the opposite sex on the lists. This process imposes a proportional vote which, moreover, is not without flaws. In an election by constituency, the most economical way would be to force voters to vote for tickets with two seats, one for each sex, so one vote for two names. Another possibility is to vote in two different electoral colleges, one male, the other female. Women elect women and men elect men. This would be going back to the organic principle of certain medieval republics, in which people voted by corporation, profession or class.

An election by vote only provides descriptive representation if the vote is tightly framed and constrained. In addition, this result is only obtained for one criterion (here gender parity). The procedural constraints of the vote will ultimately give parity, but nothing ensures a proportion of ages, incomes, residences, etc. These other criteria remain elusive. To reflect age, income or other classes, many other rules and complications would have to be introduced into the vote, which would make it very difficult to organize and which would modify the notion of free candidacy. On the contrary, without effort or constraint, sortition achieves the descriptive representation on most of the basic criteria (sex, age, income, etc.).

As we know, the referendum is the only vote which engages an entire population without distortion of representation, because it elects no one and because it mobilizes all the people instead of representing them. If it excludes the distortion of representation, the referendum can only be used for bills, ratifications or general decisions.

The descriptive effect of sortition is so great that it is found even when few people are picked from among many in a lottery process. That also applies to tiny database, as long as the chances are equal. In a population, the more the number drawn at random increases, the more descriptive the representation will be on all points.

A Sortive Democracy

After having defined the regimes by their principal procedures, we turn our attention to the democratic types according to the procedures which characterize them. From historical examples, we must either learn well-known lessons or examine possibilities that remain to be explored and tested in a new context.

The drawing of lots was essential in the first old type, because it came to consolidate and prolong the direct character of the vote in popular assembly. It was in the performance of tasks that sortition took precedence over election. The citizen performed tasks while belonging to the Council of 500 which organized the political system or while sitting, rendering the verdicts as jurors in the Popular Tribunal. In addition to the Council and the Tribunal, and this fact is even more striking in retrospect, almost all the democratically decided tasks were then carried out by citizens chosen by lot.

This is a strong incentive to put your actions in line with your words, avoiding taking decisions lightly, because there is a high probability (chances or risks) of having to carry them out yourself. Whoever decided on war will go and fight in person. Whoever has decided that this or that work is necessary will have some chance (or risk) of having to actually do this work.

As regards the execution of tasks, the draw is absent or extremely residual in the second modern type. Does a sortition-based regime constitute a type of democracy in its own right? Historically maybe not, but theoretically yes. Maybe not, because no democracy has relied solely on sortition if not, to make fun of it, in a comedy by Aristophanes (*Women in the Assembly*). Theoretically yes, because a third type of democracy emerges from historical comparisons: a sortive democracy centred on the advantages of the draw.

As we have seen, the draw as an operation and sortition as a procedure have the advantage of easily contributing to the two forms of representation. There is no doubt about sortition's ability to be descriptive. However, its potential for active representation is not negligible. Nothing even prevents drawing from a database external to the population to be represented. A lawyer can be drawn by lot from a base of qualified lawyers without being part of the potential base of defendants.

A third type of democracy must be identified because it does not exactly match the characteristics of the other two: it is neither indirect nor direct. The legitimate objection to its existence and its definition is that it has never constituted a historical experience comparable to the other two. In addition, it seems impractical on its own, without being combined with one or both of the other types. But these historical types themselves never appear in a pure and perfect version. While this third type does not weigh as heavily as the other two, it is precisely the ability to combine it that makes it interesting. Intended to be associated, this third type of democracy is much more extensive, flexible and varied than one might first imagine. It does not reproduce the opposition between direct and indirect and tends to substitute an opposition between active and inactive.

If sortition is used to entrust executive tasks, to constitute colleges of decision-makers, controllers or users, it favours a wide, continuous and effective participation, which recalls the participatory character of the first democratic type. Otherwise, if it is used, by a rigorous sampling process, to add a descriptive dimension to the active representation practised in the second type of democracy, it achieves a better representation by combining the active and descriptive aspects. Strong point: it changes the democratic situation and makes it more intense. Weak point: it remains to be tested in terms of effective participation, acceptance of assigned tasks, evaluation of their own activity by the officials chosen by lot. Its positive contribution to the overall democratic procedure has to be assessed.

Will sortition prove to be in line with expectations? How do you know before you try it? Exercising active citizenship, at the level of local or national politics as in any appropriate institution, is a plausible goal if the draw is well operated and sortition is understood and used deftly. We can hope that this usage provides one of the urgent remedies for the decadence of political activity now transformed into a superficial spectacle.

Among other qualities, sortive democracy is distinguished by its specific approach to equality. A principle of equality based on the equal chance of being selected is very different from the principles of equality invoked in other types of democracy. In the indirect type, equality is above all an equal right to designate your representative and the leader. In the direct type, equality is an equal right to participate in decision-making, in passing laws, but rarely in their execution.

Equality through the drawing of lots opens up other fields. Respect for the proportions of the population in a truly descriptive sample is a guarantee of equality, passive for the population, active for the members of the group formed by sortition. The draw brings the idea that equal rights and the chance to be chosen to act or represent are not always contradictory. In general, voting is a low intensity right/duty, honour/ chore. These two aspects are taken much further by the lottery. The practical implication and the lively consequences are often much higher if we compare the person chosen by lot to a voter.

On a very large scale, the use of a large-scale drawing is generally democratic at the level of universal suffrage, even hyper-democratic, for example if a thousand people are chosen by lot to bring them together in a consultative national assembly. In contrast, for military service, the same equality of opportunity achieved on a large scale is, for the majority of those concerned, closer to a duty or sacrifice than to a chance of performing the task.

Like voting, the draw allows participation at all levels. Its use goes beyond the political sphere and extends to social, cultural and academic activities. The essential quality of sortition is that it achieves a specific equality at the level at which it is performed. We have to be careful, however: the real equality of chances at the practised level says nothing about its meaning at the higher level. A very elitist group can use the lottery in a democratic way inside without ceasing to be elitist, even anti-democratic outside, in relation to its environment. This nuance reminds us that procedures have no political essence but only properties given by their material operation and the rules that frame them.

Sortition entails often more equality than other procedures at its level of practice. This does not mean that this body will contribute to democracy or to equality in the system which encompasses it. A lottery can be used by any type of organization, from the least to the most elitist. This does not mean that this equality is fairer either, because this last point depends on the situation and the purpose of the procedure and not on its material operation. In this area, we should not confuse small numbers with elitism. A prior competence test is the *sine qua non* of a selection for a specialized function. Consider mathematicians, marathon runners, violinists or pole vaulters: before a random selection of individuals from among all of them, it is necessary to know by a test that these people have the required qualification for the task or the academic, musical or sporting function required. It is not elitism, meritocracy, but simple consistency. If the function requires the practice of Japanese language, the base must obviously be reduced to this capable set. When the function does not require any particular quality, it is no longer necessary to limit the base, at least if it is the broadest principle of equality that justifies the use of sortition.

The draw defines a sortive democracy. Voting does not define a particular type, because it is used differently in direct and indirect types. No democracy could do without voting, while a democracy is conceivable without sortition. Defining this sortive type apart does not mean isolating it, on the contrary.

It is important to distinguish this third type of democracy precisely because the draw is not always democratic. It contributes to a kind of democracy only under certain conditions in its operation, its conception and its purpose. Democracy does not require the draw. The drawing of lots is not always democratic. As a procedure, sortition, just like the five others defined (see chapter 1), it is available to all regimes, from democracy to tyranny.

The three types defined according to their main procedure (direct, indirect, sortive) include subtypes. The first subtype, *indirect representative*, centres on a quasi-sovereign parliament and the succession of clearly identified parliamentary majorities. The historical source and purest type is the United Kingdom. The Federal Republic of Germany gives a very attenuated version of this by the use of semi-proportional voting and the habitual practice of large national coalitions.

The second subtype, *indirect*, is based on the separation and balance of power. It is ensured by the Constitution of the United States. A combined subtype on intermittent mode exists in the French Constitution: the presidency and the legislative power, both elected, prevail over the other, depending on the political balance of power. The preponderance of the presidency has so far been more common than the parliamentarism of "cohabitation".

In direct democracy, a first direct subtype includes any system giving a final say to the popular vote by referendum. In various ways, important laws are or can be submitted for popular ratification, by government choice or by petition about a law passed in parliament. A second subtype also grants a first word through the popular initiative, a legal petition leading to a popular consultation. It took Switzerland dozens of years to pass from the first to the second type.

The first sortive subtype is marked by a strong emphasis on equalizing procedures, whether it is about equality of opportunity or even equality of constraints by the draw. Athens has never been equalled on this point since the word "democracy" was created. The second subtype of sortive democracy is more oriented towards neutralization, impartiality, anti-partisan procedures. An aristocratic republic like Venice used the lottery for these purposes.

The frog of sortition will never be as big as the ox of democracy. Before presenting the practical details of the lottery in politics, I will examine its uses and purposes by summarizing them in a typology.

Chapter 3

Main Uses

To varying degrees, at different times and in different contexts, the lottery has been used for the following purposes, simultaneously or not: for the rotation of functions, for allocating resources, objects, budget or items, for sampling or representation, for selecting people by lot to perform a task or function.

Task Rotation and Rotation of Individuals

To run through all types of attribution (task, function, use of an object, speaking time, etc.) the drawing of lots organizes the passage of all, or almost all, in turn. This involves spreading out identical tasks or functions over time.

Applied to the same function, the principle of rotation implies that the person who has been chosen is no longer part of the database after having been selected once. Thus the degree of rotation is maximum. When the duration of the duties is short, these duties are specified at the time of the draw. When the offices are regularly held for a year or more, a draw for new office-holders is made before each deadline. Such was the dynamic of the Athenian system. The only permanent faculty or function consisted of voting in a popular assembly about twenty times a year during a citizen's life. The other two situations were complementary and intermittent (or reversible over time). It involved being in turn ruler (essentially executing) or governed (citizen obeying the laws and the magistrates responsible for enforcing them).

One of the objectives of such reversibility is a long apprentice-ship in democracy. So everyone changes roles, knows and lives the difficulties and details of each situation. This type of reversi-bility has disappeared from modern societies, or rather it is only passive and limited: today the pedestrian and the driver are often the same person living both situations, alternating the two roles according to the need of the moment. We learn in this rotation that a green or red light does not constitute an obstacle to freedom of movement, but a limit required by a common interest. This very simple example clearly shows that a citizen will better respect a law understood as a sharing of roles and from which each person benefits doubly when passing from one role to another.

The rotation of functions is inspired by the precept "do not treat others as you would not want them to treat you". Machiavelli underlined that the condition of any republican and democratic policy was that the governed judge the policy by putting himself in the place of the ruler. A republic, he said, is impossible if citizens behave like passive customers waiting to be served. The exchange of roles, through an Athenian-type rotation, responds to this concern and attempts to fulfil this republican condition. One day a citizen is controlled by the police, the other day this citizen is a police officer controlling other citizens, so that everyone must obey the law in both roles.

At lower intensity, on secondary but not insignificant aspects, the rotation by sortition is impartial in the allocation of speaking times and time slots. Candidates for an exam take the test in the order determined by the draw. During national elections in France, the broadcasts and speaking times of candidates or parties are drawn. The same instrument is very useful for organizing sessions of deliberation, negotiation or consultation.

A rotation of participation made by the draw does not fall under the representative principle, since all are, have been or will be in office. This is why a draw, in its political or professional sense, is at the opposite extreme of a raffle. In the rotation, everyone ends up passing (winning?). A lottery in which the prize was awarded to everyone in turn would have nothing of what is usually understood as a raffle, where the prize is huge and the chance of winning is tiny.

Allocation of a Good or Item

This way of allocating at random is often used to avoid auction and competition, it is also against any pre-established merit criteria (hierarchical position, tradition) that the lottery is used when allocating a property. It withdraws the social, economic or other benefits.

In our bureaucratic societies mostly devoted to trade, the allocation of goods and resources is dominated by market and test procedures, while leaving room for inheritance in the transmission of goods. The drawing of lots, rare in this allocation process, has a great impact when it is combined with market. It is used to allocate apartments in the same residence. It is used for preparing shares in an inheritance.

Its use does not imply free access. The items or goods drawn may have a fixed price for all potential buyers. What is ruled out is the auction. Any rise in prices is impossible or contained. If demand greatly exceeds supply, a paid ticket may be awarded by drawing from among all buyers. Lotteries allocating tickets for the Olympic Games, concerts, fishing licences are common examples. This type of random allocation takes on a more political and egalitarian turn for visas, work permits or immigration rights, for example in Green Card (long-term visa) applications in the United States.

In France, the lottery has been used to register students from among the number of applicants with a strong excess of demand in certain university courses. In October 2017, court decisions condemned this practice. The French government now prohibits such sortition by default. It is indeed fairer to grant a year of study to students who are best prepared by their academic results, by demonstrating their knowledge and their motivations. Under the pretext of equal access, avoiding any assessment of knowledge here is arbitrary, lazy and, on the whole, incompatible with the collective interest and individual merit as well.

We can imagine teaching without grading, without exams, without rankings. This is a better option in some cases. The idea of drawing lots for grading and awarding grades is absurd.

The allocation of a good or item by drawing lots is radically different from all other forms of allocation. It sometimes presupposes a qualification (one will attribute an instrument only to the person able to play) or a purchase (the drawing coming to decide between the buyers). The most common case today is probably experienced when awarding tickets.

Sampling and Survey

The use of random selection to obtain a representative sample of the population is invaluable for polls, sociological studies, political or business simulations. The very good descriptive representation provided by the lottery could be used more, but quota methods often cost less.

As we have seen, a sample drawn at random, above a rather modest threshold, gives the exact proportions of a population and can therefore be used, for example, in surveys aimed at predicting consumption behaviour or vote. If the target level of precision is medium, 100 to 200 people drawn at random from the entire French population are sufficient. If one aims for a higher degree, then allowing very reliable predictions, 1,000 to 9,000 individuals drawn at random from a population of several tens of millions provide the necessary sample. In France, the confidence interval (or margin of error) is 1.4% for a sample of 5,000 people among the entire electorate (Note Boy-Chiche electorate).

The proportions (in terms of age, sex, profession, habitat, etc.) of a population being well respected by the sample, it is possible to extrapolate the opinion, the vote and the behaviour of such a sample within a very small margin of error. For simple questions, particularly binary questions, the prediction of the outcome is excellent. At any scale, including small numbers, this property of the draw is promising. It is therefore unfortunate that it is only used for marketing surveys.

However, this ability to predict an outcome should not suggest replacing a national election with the use of a sample of 100,000 citizens drawn at random. Statistical and probabilistic reliability would allow it, but resorting to such a shortcut would be a bad idea for many reasons. The act of voting in a democracy has other dimensions than the simple result.

When the size of the sample is smaller, the descriptive effect decreases, but the role of the scale model remains plausible and practicable. In this sense, the constitution of a ten-person jury in a court easily selects ordinary citizens without special qualifications. Without being representative in the descriptive sense (it does not have the same proportions as the entire population), this mode of selection prevents the emergence of any dominant criterion (education, profession, age, identity) and deserves the qualifier "popular" which is generally granted.

In deliberative democracy, juries drawn by lot are entrusted as advisors. The level is most often local or regional. These are assemblies of a few tens or hundreds of people. When their proposals lead to a referendum, it compensates and erases the lack of representativeness of the group.

Selection and Nomination

It is the largest field for sortition. Its scope is immense when the base is made up of a whole population of adults, generally citizens or, in some cases, inhabitants. Each person having roughly the same competence for the general political decision (as during a vote), the qualification is granted without criteria or test before operating the draw. Lack of qualification is not a lack of registration. Registration is a first filter, and the comparison with universal suffrage remains convincing. There questions are almost the same: for example, should we be registered automatically by a bureaucracy that informs you of your registration or do we need to take steps to be properly registered?

In contrast, a draw combined with election applies very well to a very small number of people previously qualified by a test or any other sort of criterion having formed a small set of people of approximately equal competence. Its essential quality is that no objection of capability or competence shall be opposed to the draw provided it has been preceded by an appropriate qualification.

If we need a pole vaulter jumping 3 metres regularly, we will first look to list a database of pole vaulters. We can select any practising pole vaulter who has already cleared 4 metres and the lottery will designate one or more pole vaulters able to jump 3 metres in due time (soon).

Another solution: we can carry out a test offered to all volunteers. It will then suffice to designate one or more individuals from among those who crossed 4 metres during the test. We will be sure that they will all be able to jump 3 metres under normal conditions.

All the differences and nuances that sortition allows are affirmed in the historical examples already mentioned and can be seen very clearly in the proposals that will be made in the last chapter of this book.

Chapter 4

Misleading Conceptions

Sortition, as a procedure and like any procedure, cannot be reduced to an essence, a single effect or a single goal. It cannot by itself embody democracy or equality or impartiality, but only contribute to their practice. However, supporters and opponents of sortition sometimes give in to the temptation to reduce this type of selection to an unequivocal generality. It is better to give up certain illusions and quickly clarify, against many preconceived ideas, what sortition is not. Its effects are too diverse to be reduced to a single characteristic.

Randomness

The most common association of ideas, ubiquitous in debates over selection by lot, is the assimilation of sortition to pure randomness. This is to confuse the operation and the procedure. The operation materializes and realizes the randomness of the result, but the procedure only uses chance for purposes other than itself.

It is true that an individual chosen by lot for a representative sample is at his or her individual level of probability actually chosen at random. The overall result is nevertheless quite the opposite of chance. It is the greatest possible statistical precision which is sought here. Chance becomes a precision statistical tool to obtain a very representative sample.

From one draw to the next, when the people selected by lottery change, the proportions remain. Chance plays a role only on the scale of the chosen individual. In this process, the individual is designated by the draw to represent and not to be distinguished as an individual. A mirror does not reflect a random image. A reduced model even makes it possible, by the non-random accumulation of individuals drawn at random, to reconstruct by deduction a population of the whole in its main characteristics when we do not know it. Likewise, and when the draw is used for rotations, chance concerns only the moment of the passage. Achieving it in the near or distant future is a certainty when there is total rotation in the group.

To claim that using sortition is to prefer chance over other criteria is, in most cases, an absurdity. Sortition, as an operation and a procedure, does not in itself worship or deify randomness, since the procedure uses the operation for purposes of representation, modelling, rotation. And if necessary, in the selection by lot, the preoperative qualification does eliminate what could have remained hazardous in the procedure.

We should renounce any term or concept of "power of chance" to define sortition ("stochocracy", for example). The fact of not being able to predict the fates of the individuals of the base before the draw is wanted, even necessary. We accept this use of hazard only for certain purposes and we do not seek to strengthen, increase or multiply it in any way.

By the way, going places at random during a walk is not about drawing lots at every crossroads. To wander, all you have to do is not pay too much attention to the options that present themselves, moving forward a little mechanically or absent-mindedly. The walk becomes random. The draw, on the contrary, equalizes the options to make a choice operational. It works as an organizer.

If I compose a text by picking randomly each word after word in a dictionary, I get an unintelligible text. The draw, though very real, nevertheless amounts to a negation of any procedure. Its outcome is nothing more than a chaotic result or, at best, the surprise of a few random encounters with unwanted meaning. The expectation was to have no meaningful results. Under these conditions, producing a coherent sentence is a small miracle, obtained in spite of the operation, against it, in spite of the fact of having picked words at random.

Pick ten words at random from the entire dictionary. Repeat the operation and see how many prints it will take to have an intelligible sequence. Some results will be pleasing because of their fancy and not because of their practicality. When viewed closely, the association of sortition and randomness is not and cannot be the goal of sortition in politics and its other social uses, unless that goal is unlimited disorganization.

Randomness is very real when you use a lottery to choose a decision from among different options, but that is hardly ever what is involved when sortition is used in politics. Let's go even further: there is more hazard in a presidential election than in most uses of the lottery in politics. A presidential election opposing a few personalities is a crossroads of personal destinies and unpredictable events. As for the jackpot games, the practice of drawing lots consists of discreetly raising a disguised tax and nurturing the hope of extraordinary wealth among the poor, dreamers or discontented.

Divine Will

Relying on the gods' will while using a sacred lottery is common in polytheism. It is less frequent or sometimes prohibited in monotheism. The Bible mentions little use of the draw. In most societies which make use of a sacred lottery, it is difficult to distinguish between religion, superstition and divination. Today, the use of sortition is not or is no longer a matter of mystique, supernatural belief.

There is a paradox in the two perspectives: if one does not believe in the divine character of the lottery, the divine will is only a word placed on the contingency or the necessity (known or unknown) of an event. On the other hand, if we believe in it, then it is some chance that does not exist and cannot exist since the apparent contingency of the result is explained by a supernatural will.

The question also arises in these terms: did the inventors of the lottery believe in its divine character? Before the creation of democratic rule, the use of the lottery in archaic Greece was more religious than political, and if it became political in addition, in any case it was not related to democracy. Any regime could use such a sacred lottery. It could be used for taking decisions, for attributing liturgical functions. It was in a second step that the lottery was turned into some democratic device by some daring reformers.

There is, however, no serious reason to oppose these two aspects of sortition *a posteriori*. Under democratic rule, some drawings of lots were made in the sacred solemnity of Athenian temples, others in machines, more routinely. Political use complemented religious use. The new political significance does not prevent the previous one from remaining as the (perhaps sacred) solemnity of the operation, nor does the earlier religious significance preclude its subsequent political use.

If the lottery in Athenian democracy had been primarily a religious fact, such a careful observer as Aristotle would have insisted on this aspect of the procedure. Aristotle speaks of social, political, psychological causes when he studies sortition. If fate determined by the draw has become a political means in the service of democracy, there is nothing to prove that it has ceased to be a religious symbol. But, conversely, if sortition was only employed out of a desire to conform to the will of the gods, why else would such a regime give the main power to a popular assembly? An assembly of priests would have been much better.

There is nothing contradictory about the practice of a lottery that is political and religious as well. The disjunction of these two orders is somewhat rare in the history of mankind, especially in antiquity. We should not simplify the question by contrasting everything religious with everything political. It is true that in today's curiosity for the ancient lottery being mainly political and democratic, we tend to consider only this political aspect. It is not necessary, however, to be a democrat to postulate that the lottery had, in Athenian democracy, lost all religious aspect. The point of the democratic argument for the lottery is that this religious aspect is not the main one. Once again we verify our starting point: sortition is not democratic in essence, simply because no procedure is one and only one thing. That being said, the reform of Cleisthenes was intended to democratize the aristocratic Athenian political system, in particular through the increased use of the lottery. This reform loosened the sacred bond with religion. Even more, it broke clan and family ties by creating a purely territorial civil status.

Democracy made sortition more political than religious. The civic spirit inherent in the practice of drawing lots could nevertheless incorporate these two meanings without contradiction. We do not, however, infer from the sacred oath taken by the President of the United States that clerics rule in Washington. Religious beliefs are present, but do not dominate the administration. In this sense, sortition remained all the more religious in Athens because its religion was a religion of the city, a cult of protective divinities as political and powerful as they were mystical, such as Athena.

Greek religion can hardly be compared with the modern idea of religion. Perhaps this religion was more democratic than sacred since it was allowed to make fun of the gods in the comedy contests accompanying the festivals given in their name, as evidenced by the theatre of Aristophanes. The Greek gods live almost human passions, quarrel, play bad tricks. The will of such gods manifests itself in the register of human passions: seduction, anger, jealousy, revenge.

Other times, other customs: in the Christian context of medieval Italian cities, no religious dogma favourable to the lottery justified its practice. Sortition was tolerated by the Catholic Church as a specifically political procedure. It was valued or criticized for its advantages and disadvantages in the political system.

A Regenerative Utopia

Overvaluation is another avenue to be avoided. It is illusory to make a procedure (sortition or any other one) a solution in itself. A lottery-based procedure, like any procedure, is too flexible and variable to be the key to a system on its own. Its use can be revolutionary or conservative, stabilizing or chaotic, representative or not, liberating or oppressive, predictable or unpredictable. It would not be enough to generalize sortition to change everything in a political system. The impact would certainly be great, but there are several types of sortition and their effects go in different directions depending on the details of procedure.

Assuming that sortition realizes democracy is like believing that the election of a parliament is enough to make a representative democracy. The existence of a legal and protected opposition is far more important, among other things, than the fact of bringing together members of parliament in a chamber. Hemicycles full of supposed delegates and huge convention centres are frequent in authoritarian regimes.

Likewise, the practice of referendums is not enough to create a direct democracy or a democracy at all. Without many guarantees (information, free discussion, rule of law, absence of pressure), a referendum is mostly a plebiscite against a backdrop of demagoguery or terror.

The same reasoning obviously applies to the drawing of lots. Fascist, communist or variously oppressive dictatorships can or will use it, provided they manipulate the procedure. And even setting aside these manipulations, and assuming that sortition is perfectly used for all its benefits and without corruption of any kind, will it be the solution on its own? No, to believe in the unique and universal solution, whether it be religious, political, moral or economic, whether it be procedure, regime or way of life, is utopian, simplistic, and often violent. On the other hand, the use of sortition will be all the more effective as we take the trouble to measure what it can, but also what it cannot and never will be able to provide.

There is another utopian vision of sortition: the social lottery. This temptation was at least thought and imagined since the drawing of lots exists in a procedure. It was ridiculed by Aristophanes in *Women in the Assembly*. In a more serious and modernized version, in *Justice by Lottery*, Barbara Goodwin proposes the drawing of lots for professions in our societies. It is utopian in the strict sense: every citizen gets a job by lot. Several jobs will be assigned to an individual in a lifetime, regardless of rank, education or wealth. A training for this future job will be provided. This is a society in which equality of opportunity results from the drawing of lots. Rotation in multiple professions compensates for any unfairness in the assignment. In turn, worker, farmer, employee, manager, each person embodies the whole of society. There are undoubtedly limits and some very difficult professions must be tested. But nobody will exercise them exclusively. The surgeon will not only be a surgeon and the mathematician will have the chance to do a little manual work. It is very interesting to see where limits are placed in this thought experiment. In Barbara Goodwin's lottery society, children and their education are not randomly selected.

The practical problems (training, fraud, exception, consent) that such a system would create would have to be examined very precisely. As much as imagining the ideal of a political regime, this utopia suggests a way to overcome the failure of egalitarian revolutions that have proceeded by statization, dictatorship, expertise and planning. Egalitarianism is postponed and based on the effects of sortition. It is not its so-called intrinsically democratic character that is put forward, but its incredible extension, its implacable generalization in social, professional and cultural life. This rotation of roles, pleasures and pains, powers and duties, would indeed be revolutionary, egalitarian, sometimes disturbing, communist of a whole new type. This contribution to the genre of the ideally just city, a noble genre since Plato and Thomas More, shows to what extent the use of the lottery is not only political but can become moral, social, psychological. There are ideas to be gleaned from such a utopia. It does not define sortition as a procedure.

Competence and Incompetence

The last misconception is the one that usually comes first to mind when discussing a possible sortition. Supporters and opponents of the use of the lottery often clash over this question of competence. Yet this is a false problem.

Resorting to sortition, for some, would be the recognition of a democratic competence intrinsic to any human group. For their opponents, it would be the most total demagoguery in action, a blind egalitarianism insensitive to any difference in knowledge, skill, experience in the conduct of business (political or otherwise). If there are differences in the skills required by function, the definition of the database allows an adjustment. This is necessary in all procedures: a qualified legal database is needed for a vote. Access to the market or registering for an exam, in most cases, also involves membership in a qualified base. However, if the function to which one can be chosen by lot requires a very specialized skill, it will have been tested before during the registration of the base. In cases of less specialization required, it will have been necessary to think about the adequacy between the draw and the functions to adjust the base. This adjustment does not come up against any insurmountable obstacle. The solution lies in the many and diverse forms of qualification.

To dispel this obsession with incompetence, examples are revealing. I certainly wouldn't want a tooth pulled out by an individual randomly selected from among the population. The absurdity of the suggestion lies in its consequences, just as I wouldn't want to have been designated to pull a tooth out of anyone when I haven't mastered the technique. Let's call it proof by the dentist.

To establish the competence in the matter of sortition, therefore, it is not necessary to refer to the account of Protagoras set forth by Plato in the dialogue of the same name. No need to take sides with Protagoras or Plato or Socrates. The existence of equal human capacity (according to Protagoras) in the given moral and political judgement (Protagoras's pro-democracy thesis) holds for political judgement in general and democratic decision-making in particular. This judgement does not depend on technical training. It can be improved by experience, usage, intelligence, education, but always as a generality. And no training guarantees progress in moral and political judgement, whereas, in technical matters, learning always gives a more or less advanced competence. There are great differences in performance between swimmers, but the radical separation of competence is between swimmers and those who cannot swim. On the contrary, every person is endowed with the capacity to judge morally and politically his own experience of life and society, to feel justice and injustice, to measure freedom and constraint and to interpret any other social and moral fact.

The frequent debate on general competence therefore only makes sense in cases where no qualification is retained. As regards sortition, it is when the database is as wide as possible, without qualification. But in this case, the issue of competence is the same for voting, association, inheritance and a few other procedures. This aspect is not unique to sortition. If it is mentioned much more frequently about it, it is for a lack of thought and experience.

The examination of many details in the second part of this book will confirm that on the competence and incompetence of those subjected to sortition, the solution is obvious in practice and the problem superfluous in theory.

Chapter 5

Effects and Objectives

The operation of the lottery is the equivalent of the musical instrument, while the procedure is the music itself. The instrument must be suitable for the type of music. The goal is more important than the operation, since it is the political or moral motive of the procedure. However, operating correctly is of the utmost importance.

The usual effects of a lottery are: impartiality, simplicity, integration, serenity, equality. These effects, partly expected from the operation itself, are incorporated into the finality of the proceedings if the details have been appropriately worked out. The draw tends in general, in most cases, to simplify the procedures. It saves time, resources, energy and calculations. It is an effect of simplicity. No simplification is always reliable. It remains to verify that this purpose has been achieved in accordance with expectations.

Not all types of lotteries are listed and studied here. We limit ourselves to those who have a political purpose, the word political being taken in the broad sense: the organization of societies and groups from a procedural angle. These purposes are representation, participation, deliberation, decision-making, democratization, appeasement, lack of intrigue, prevention of corruption.

The Usual Effects

Impartiality

This almost mechanical effect is the first and most specific of a random selection. No drawing of lots gives rise to an open competition between persons or parties. No one can side with someone else to try to tip the scales. The operation of the lottery materially prevents the formation of coalitions, factions, winning or losing strategies, interventions, influences outside of the process. Manoeuvres, intrigues, campaigns are impossible. Only hardware fraud remains a threat.

A lottery thus serves to neutralize or eliminate all preparations, anticipations, calculations and acts of influence. If five people have to be chosen out of a hundred, no preparation to determine the outcome of the operation will be possible. Nobody makes the choice. Only the operation is performed. This choice therefore escapes conflicts of interest. As Oliver Dowlen rightly observes, this property of sortition is "a-rational" (in *The Political Potential of Sortition*, 2008).

In comparison, electing people through a vote involves publicity, competition, struggle for influence, a coalition of supporters and, too often, rumours and lies as numerous as sincere and disinterested arguments. This aspect of elective voting is found even in a reduced form in a vote without a candidate, in which the competition related to the candidacy is absent or less intense, but the choice nevertheless made through consultations, calculations and intentions. An implicit campaign opens *de facto* in the (rare) votes without candidates.

This impartiality, neutralizing effect is all the more important since, on this point, it clearly distinguishes the drawing of lots from other procedures. Manoeuvre, intrigue, more or less honest communication, interference, power games, exchanges of service, hidden or ostensible support often precede the decisive operation in the other possible procedures (vote, market and, to a lesser extent, test, membership). Conversely, conquering ambition and calculated manoeuvre have no place or meaning in a draw. Ambition boils down to hoping for good luck.

You can only win or lose in a draw in the least competitive sense possible, which means without an opponent and without a fight. Most often, only the person chosen by lot will be able to say whether they consider themselves a winner or a loser, depending on whether it is good news for them (honour, responsibility, activity, curiosity) or bad news (drudgery, embarrassment, danger, loss of time). The draw only produces winners and losers if it is preceded by nominations and, in this case, it is a victory in the most toned down and devalued sense of the word. All defeat is devoid of the feeling of being inferior and the feeling of injustice.

When the procedure includes a first phase of selecting people from the base, this moment of the procedure can be a competition leading to a vote or a co-option. The whole procedure then combines several operations in a sequence, in which the crucial moment is the draw. The operation is not affected in its mechanism by the effect of the qualification carried out during the first phase. Impartiality remains intact at the most decisive moment.

Simplicity and economy

The effect of simplicity is a very strong characteristic of the lottery. Compared to a vote or a test, the draw is more economical on most points. This requires little preparation, once the database is listed. The drawing operation is done quickly. Getting the result is much less difficult, in terms of calculation, than counting many ballots.

The saving of time, the weak mobilization, the light preparation and the small financial cost are ultimately an individual and collective energy saving. This is one of the reasons why a draw is sometimes used by default due to lack of resources. The economy of means specific to the operation has repercussions on the entire procedure. The financing and costs of an election campaign, advertising campaign, lobbying or communication are far beyond the cost of a lottery. This is especially true *ex ante*. *Ex post*, the procedure is not always the most economical. Sometimes it is necessary to train the persons selected by lot for their future task. Selection by test is often more economical on this point. Everything here depends on the basis of the draw: large or small, little or very qualified.

Materializing a body politic

A direct democracy achieves the full integration of the entire body politic. Whether as a group of active citizens in a popular assembly or as an electorate in a referendum, all are encouraged or even forced to participate. The draw does not really mobilize at this stage. It virtually integrates people into a database and then concerns them concretely by involving as many people as possible in the sortition procedure. The participation achieved by the draw remains of the order of an expectation, as luck or chore. The pressure exerted on the individual by a possible participation obviously depends on the degree of probability of being selected.

This dynamic of integration creates a situation of expectation and availability in the population concerned, at least in many individuals and groups. It is true that it does not create the unique space-time of a voting day, but it allows for a less ephemeral and less transient feeling of belonging to arise when the draws are repeated and cover many subjects, in various fields. Being registered in various sortition bases, in various places, for various activities, creates a kind of full-fledged body politic.

The integration practised as a permanent availability and a possible chance to serve is something latent and potential for the majority of those concerned. It becomes effective and certain if a rotation exists. Without rotation of all or almost all, belonging to a sortition base is at least comparable to registering on a voters list. It encourages people to be informed, to follow events, to prepare for action. This incentive to be informed involves a factor heavier than in the vote: the possibility for all to be chosen by lot so that they have to take office. The task at hand is less generalized and much less easy than just going to vote. It mobilizes attention just as much and differently, because the task will be more demanding, intense and time-consuming if fate so decides.

The mere fact of having a chance to take on a task affects almost the entire population. This form of integration is therefore very different from the one achieved through electoral participation. Its contextual impact means that no one is marginalized. The trust placed and the responsibility given in the event are more important than the repercussions of a right to vote. They are more interesting, sometimes more disturbing too. Anyone is alerted by the possibility of being chosen by lot.

Obviously, this alert effect varies with the probability of being chosen by lot, whether it is large or small. You feel more susceptible to be selected if the probability is 1/5th or 1/10th and much less if it is 1/10,000 or 1/100,000.

A guarantee of serenity

"The draw is a way of electing that does not grieve anyone", writes Montesquieu in *De l'esprit des lois*, 1748, book II, chapter3 (*Le sort est une façon d'élire qui n'afflige personne*). The possible disappointment of not having been chosen by lot cannot engender bitterness or resentment. No person responsible for failure or success can be named. The operation is innocent. The unselected or the disappointed are not vanquished or expelled. They are not losers nor victims. This is an incentive to participate without having to fight for a nomination or an election. The drawing of lots does not authorize the winner to claim victory either. The draw does not flatter anyone. It defuses the pride of the chosen one. It withdraws all pretensions of superiority. Luck is not distributed evenly, but it does equalize feelings and protect self-esteem. The drawing of lots mitigates arrogance: there is no reason to scorn those who have not been elected. You can only rely on luck. Sometimes that is enough for the lucky one to feel important, but it is not in the name of merit.

The unselected therefore has no hard feelings. Bitterness can only be exercised against due process. Perhaps we would have preferred to see other people selected instead of the selected ones. However, the operation did not create personal antagonism. The procedure calms passions. Resentment towards the winner would be absurd. Self-criticism as a loser does not make much sense either. Only jealousy remains possible.

For these reasons, the effect of serenity complements the effect of impartiality. This removes the suspicion of interference and favouritism. Equalization of opportunity creates a sense of fairness. This psychological effect is general: it is found among the chosen ones as in the rest of the population. Its impact is individual and collective.

Montesquieu's remark noted this overall effect. No one is distressed, touched, bruised or shocked by the result. This goes even for an observer who does not belong to the base or to the population in which the base is qualified. We must therefore add: sortition accuses no one. If I watch a draw, the injustice will only come from a fraud. Happy or disappointed with the result, I can only congratulate or curse the good luck or bad luck.

The serenity induced by the draw therefore manifests itself in many places and in several dimensions. It is psychological, social and political. Its contribution to peace, calm and equity is made through concrete, almost forced detachment. Freeing oneself from passions here requires no moral effort. The suspicion can only relate to the regularity of the operation. The degree of adversity is at its lowest.

Equality Issues

The drawing of lots equalizes the chances of all the people subjected to its operation, provided that these chances are not weighted: each person has a single ticket, one name is equivalent to a single name or number. This egalitarian effect occurs at the level where the transaction is performed. This is true regardless of the size of the base, whether a few individuals, thousands or millions.

There may be good reasons for balancing a draw by giving some individuals more chances than others, but this is a choice of procedure, a finality leading to combine operations. Sometimes for the sake of fairness, based on pre-existing data, a draw will be weighted by attributing, whatever the criterion, more chances to certain individuals than to others. This exception confirms the rule of equal opportunity. Few draws are weighted. Let us leave aside the very special case in which one person may have a higher number of chances than another by buying more tickets. The market procedure here interferes with sortition.

However, we must distinguish the egalitarian effect from the democratic effect. The two overlap but do not coincide. Any equalization of opportunities is not democratic and is not sufficient to define democracy as a political regime or a social situation. If a tyrant decides to use the lottery to imprison or kill a percentage of the population in order to terrorize the rest, the process will not be considered democratic. Yet the operation meets a criterion of equality if the odds are equal and the operation without fraud. Such a difference between equality and democracy is found in many less tragic cases.

It is not only for the sake of equality that a democratic regime tends to use the lottery. The previously observed effects are necessary in a democracy worthy of the name. However, only the political context of a democracy worthy of the name transforms the intrinsic equalization of the lottery into a democratic procedure. The equality of all except one under the empire of a tyrant, Montesquieu noted, unfortunately exists and is detestable. Equality without freedom is a dubious good to say the least. The same applies to the egalitarian use of the lottery. For a drawing of lots to be democratic, it is therefore necessary to have carried out the operation correctly: it must be fair, with the proper degree of qualification and without fraud. Then give it a purpose that respects the fundamental principles of democracy, which goes far beyond achieving equal opportunities. Equal opportunity to be terrorized is not democratic.

Moreover, a very meritocratic organization may have an inherent advantage in introducing sortition in its ruling group (or in different specific cells or departments of its structure), it remains that its oligarchic or aristocratic nature as a whole will not be affected. Its solidity may even be reinforced if this internal process allows the group to be better united, more cooperative, more efficient, more devoted to the institution.

Likewise, with regard to the draw, the effect of egalitarian justice with a limited scope (or a very specific activity), otherwise indifferent or even hostile to global justice, has been known for a long time: pirates, thieves, gangs often use the draw to assign roles, distribute prebends or share loot. This fact is often over-looked by some advocates of sortition, so tempted to place the lottery operation in an immaculate procedural sphere.

The main democratic point is the equalizing effect of the draw as an operation well controlled at its procedural level. Defining the appropriate proportion between those number of people selected and the size of the base is essential. The extension or restriction of this proportion must be assessed on a case-by-case examination. The question consists precisely in finding the opti-mal fit in each case. This scale begins, as we have seen, at the level of universal suffrage and decreases in size to restricted levels where the draw involves only a few people.

Political Goals

The main political purposes of contemporary uses of sortition are, according to the functions for which it is intended or according to those it fulfils: *representation, participation, deliberation, decision, democratization, appeasement, prevention of corruption*. The success of the procedure must be analysed on two levels. Does the perform-ance of the selected official or the group resulting from the draw meet expectations? Is the expected systemic contribution achieved at the level of the institution? The typical examples presented in the following chapters will give an overview of some possibilities.

Democratization is measured in the composition and functioning of the groups, colleges and organizations drawn by lot and then in their impact on their institutional and social environment. Democratization is to obtain more equality, freedom, consultation, cooperation, collective decision-making, civic-mindedness, a sense of the general interest, respect for rules and laws. Using the draw is interesting if these results are on average higher than they would have been without resorting to the draw.

The main problem lies in the operation and results of a randomly selected body. The objectives of participation and representation are objectives already partially achieved as soon as the lottery is set up, as we saw in the first two chapters. Likewise, the organization of a referendum automatically increases the scope and degree of citizen participation in political deliberations and decision-making. This does not prejudge or predict the quality of the result, in terms of decision or legislation.

As in a vote, but with more intensity and importance, the question of obligation arises: to belong or not to belong to the database? Should we or should we not be obliged to accept the function assigned by the procedure if we have been selected by the draw?

Election by vote encourages patronage, partisan arrangements and the pursuit of perpetual re-election. In contrasting terms, the honesty of the draw has always been recognized, at least by comparison with election by vote or with hierarchical appointment. Like any procedure, the draw can be corrupted, but it remains the most difficult procedure to corrupt, both in its operation and in its psychological effects on the selected officials by the draw and on the rest of the population. The effect of impartiality therefore logically led to targeting a related goal: the prevention of corruption. But there are limits to this reasoning. The search for an anti-corruption procedure is based on certain effects of the draw, provided that its legal basis is adequate and that the operation takes place without fraud. Second, there is no reason to infer that all the effects will be clear and one-sided. For a person as for a college, corruption is as strong a temptation for a randomly selected official as for an elected official. An elected representative of the vote is corruptible because he or she wishes to be re-elected, because he wants to consolidate his influence, because he finds support and means through lobbies or other groups of influence. Conversely, the responsibility induced by a future candidacy, the obligation to be accountable, the future campaign of the adversaries are brakes to corruption. Nothing like this hinders the person chosen by lottery: she or he will be less exposed to these positive and negative incentives. And there are other potential flaws in such a situation. She is only appointed for one term, either because a second draw is legally excluded, or, which amounts to the same thing, because the probability of being chosen by lot twice in a row is tiny. In place for a single term, this individual may however give in to the temptation to take advantage of the function. This risk is so real that the old practices of the draw have always been framed by procedures of control of the magistrates chosen by lot during their function and by the rendering of accounts at the end of their term. This proves that temptation exists, has existed, will exist among those chosen by lot.

Today, would those chosen by lot prove to be less corruptible than those elected by the vote? Those chosen by lot deserve neither systematic suspicion nor "democratic" confidence. They must remain subject to precise and permanent control. This could also be done by joint bodies, resulting from various procedures. The judges and officials designated by the draw would exercise it.

Doing Away with the
Good and Bad Reasons

No purpose is common to the different types of draw. Thus, the selection of a representative sample is used for sociological surveys, opinion polls, electoral predictions, local consultation tasks, national deliberation. Sortition has, moreover, many other purposes than this descriptive representation. The common point to the various draws, if there is one, can therefore only be found in its operation and not in the procedure.

To identify this sensitive point, Oliver Dowlen coined the term "blind break", which can be defined as a "point of invisibility" or "opaque operation". This opaque operation is the result of any drawing of lots, because the draw, writes Dowlen, eliminates all possible reasons for the choice made. These are reasons, not one and single reason, this is the crucial point, because it is about eliminating both good and bad reasons. No reason, no argument can interfere with a choice by sortition. This character is particularly evident in comparison with voting, which entails many reasons, good and bad, positive and negative, for choosing one option or person over another.

This is also true with respect to procedures other than voting. Evaluating product qualities and satisfying the wishes of sellers and buyers are the driving force behind auction, market value and its adjustment, partly predictable, partly uncontrolled, with conflicting reasons and expectations. This adjustment is not the same as adding the votes or subtracting numbers from a sortition base. As for the test, it is a procedure based on an evaluation of knowledge and operational skills but also argumentative. The procedure of inheritance, although little linked to argument, combines, according to the transmission procedure, the criterion of kinship and the record of a testamentary will. The reasons for preferring one potential heir over another are often explained or explainable, even when they are not made explicit. No procedures do away with argumentative reasons as sortition does.

The drawing of lots does not allow anyone to know in advance the persons susceptible to be heirs (inheritance), nor to exchange arguments and add up wishes (vote), nor to adjust the offers and requests (market), nor to measure capacities (test), nor to register affiliations (membership). If sortition has a specific value, it is in its difference with all the other operations: it eliminates all the reasons, good or bad, which interfere in a choice. As soon as the bad reasons are likely to count for half or more, the draw becomes very interesting. By eliminating all the reasons, sortition is neither rational nor irrational, but a-rational. It must be noted finally that a-rationality characterizes the choice of options made by the selection (items or people) and not the fact of having chosen selection as a procedure. This earlier choice is part of the argument for the pros and cons of the lottery. Note in passing that it would be absurd, although possible, to use a lottery to decide whether or not to use sortition.

Peter Stone argues that the draw cleanses and moralizes politics thanks to a "sanitizing effect". I would add that the advantage of sortition can be summed up in three words or three effects: impartiality, equality, serenity.

Chapter 6

Instructions and Options

Theoretical proposals, historical studies, political considerations on sortition must have a concrete end or they are only a chimera. Being interested in procedures is not just about discovering, evaluating, describing them. It is about loving them (the word may surprise), taking care of them as a gardener takes care of his plants: knowing them, nourishing them, accompanying them. Treating procedures like delicate flowers or rare birds is far from superfluous. To forget this aspect is to stick to generalities, to ignore crucial details. In practice, a procedure often produces effects even contrary to the desired goal. Taking care also means taking seriously. To take the procedures seriously is to use them for their own merits, directly and frankly, and not for devious calculations. The referendum is often used for more than obtaining a response to carry out. It is used, politically, to gain popular consent, to divide the opposition, to capitalize on personal popularity.

Likewise, sortition can be manipulated, without taking it seriously, just to obtain tactical and political benefits. Against these threats of distortions, besides lucidity, it is the practical questions that count: knowing how to accommodate, organize, and make a procedure work is an excellent starting point.

I propose here instructions for sortition. We do need to know how to use it in the more detailed manner. Questions arise, options inevitably concern whoever wants to employ the draw as a procedure. Incidentally, this user manual helps to advance thinking.

Size of the base, duty or right to be chosen by lot, secrecy or transparency in the procedure, sanctions or rewards, frequency of operations, possible training. On all these subjects it is necessary, depending on the case, to prefer a particular procedural option. Responses must be adjusted by a pragmatic effort.

The number of elected officials to be chosen by lot depends on the purpose. This number begins with the number 1 and can go up to several thousand or even millions. When it comes to selecting more than one person, the purpose will be descriptive or not. If we want an exact descriptive representation, it suffices to follow the statistical laws to obtain the optimal size, beyond which the size of the group randomly selected would inflate too much for a small gain representing activity. If we are satisfied with a smaller sample size, for example for a small jury selected for use in court, it is because other reasons than optimal representativeness come into play: efficiency of deliberation, time saving, greater cooperation between jury members in a small group.

Once the number of people to be selected is fixed, the size of the base must be determined. Recall what was explained before, examining in detail all the options that come up at each stage of a draw. The base is the part of a population legally retained for the draw. This database lists all of the qualified people. The qualification gives the criterion defining a legal basis for people participating in a draw. Refusal of registration is the possibility for an individual not to appear in a database or to withdraw from it before the operation. Withdrawal is the possibility of relinquishing one's selection after the draw. It is done before the actual appointment for the function. Candidacy (or application) is the act of voluntary registration in a database.

Chapter 6 69

Size of Base

The size of a base can range from two individuals to a very large number. It seems technically difficult to draw lots among all living human beings at this time. This being known, provided that the specific technique makes the operation possible, the size of the base could be expanded to very large numbers, although the possibility of fraud increases with this expansion. Above all, it is a question of finding the optimal size of the base for the type of draw to be practised and the function to be fulfilled by the persons chosen by lot. After having identified a source population, it is a question, by means of a criterion, of qualifying or not persons as individuals constituting the base in which the draw will be carried out. As in a sport, any qualification has an eliminatory aspect, but unlike a sport, sortition is rarely the search for a winner.

The theoretical size of a base, it has been said, oscillates between two people and all of humanity. In most cases, the adjustment will be made from an already delimited population (city, state, association, profession, institution, organization). The existence of the source population often precedes the idea of making a draw.

The reverse path is possible. It comes down to asking: who is interested in this draw? The question invites applications or the purchase of an entry ticket to the procedure. And this question will most often be addressed to an identified population. Then the applications will produce a base of the draw.

- Option: without qualification. As a legal basis, an unqualified population is equivalent to a basis of universal suffrage. All adults having their civic rights as voters are therefore included in the procedure. The fact that they are all qualified does not mean that there is no qualification, since nationality or citizenship is required to vote in an electoral system. This means, however, that the qualification is as broad as possible, equivalent to that required to elect a parliament or vote in a referendum. However, this does not exclude a low proportion of disqualification: deprivation of civil rights, conflict of interests, previous selection by lot, for example.

• Option: with qualification. A high qualification decreases the database in a significant proportion. A criterion of social or demographic status is the most common in this case: age, profession, residence, education (diploma). The other way to reduce the base is with a test, even when it is an easy test. Anyone who succeeds is included in the database. This is a significant limitation because it requires effort to pass the test. Tests are better suited to small databases than large ones. Testing a few thousand people is no big deal. Testing a nation-wide population would amount to passing a sort of sortition permit equivalent to a driving licence. A knowledge of the fundamental elements of the political system would be comparable to the knowledge required for the highway code.

The comparison with acquiring a licence is valid if we assume that most of the people concerned want to acquire the right to register in the database, to participate in the draw, to obtain a function. It no longer makes sense if the possible task is seen as a duty or a chore. In this case, a test entails a voluntary act, a quasi-candidacy, since it is possible, voluntarily, to give incorrect answers to the questions to avoid ending up in the database and running the risk of being chosen by the draw. This refractory behaviour supposes, however, a real aversion, like a possible conscript who persists in not fulfilling the physical conditions required for military service.

• Option: applications. Opening the draw only to those who make an application strongly limits the base by the voluntary and ambitious nature of the application. Going through an application phase makes sense when skill and availability are needed. Dedication also matters in some cases. A candidacy amounts to a self-qualification. If the will and commitment are enough to qualify, the application sets the database. If a specific skill is required, the application makes a first screening, but this screening must be completed by a test or by a pre-existing diploma.

The advantage of candidacy is that a narrow base appears as soon as the first phase of the procedure. Every type of candidacy reduces the base. It is advantageous when the procedure calls for a skilled involvement. All this simplifies, legitimizes and presages an active participation in the future function.

Right or Duty

Should registration as part of the base be compulsory or optional? At what moment? What is the degree of obligation to participate? This degree can vary from 0 to 1. It depends on the general significance (political and social) attributed to the draw. Is it a right that can be claimed or disdained? Is this a duty that can only be circumvented by exception? Depending on the answers to these questions, being subject to the draw will be optional or mandatory.

- Option: application. The most facultative approach, the application is required in some cases, but goes against one of the effects and purpose of using the lottery (inclusion, inducement to participate). Applying to be included in the database is the more restricted conception of sortition. Yet despite this strong restriction, the number of candidates, in most cases, would far exceed the number of candidates in an election: there is no need to campaign, i.e. to mobilize supporters, to fight adversaries, to develop a programme and often to bear the financial cost.

- Option: withdrawal. A more moderate approach manages to combine duty and right, to balance obligation and freedom. Registration in the database is mandatory. It is impossible to escape the draw once one is qualified (*ex ante*, before the draw), but this obligation is mitigated by the possibility of declining the function in the event of selection by lot (*ex post*, after of the draw) before the nomination. The vacated place will go to the person who comes next on the list of selected individuals. The place is given to another person.

- Option: refusal (of being registered in the base). Less restrictive from the start, this option allows a refusal to register in the database before the draw. It is allowed to decline the registration in the base when the registration is notified to the person concerned.
- Option: obligation. In this case, the obligation is total. No prior refusal (non-registration) and no withdrawal is accepted, with very few exceptions (illness, physical or mental incapacity).

Five-point recapitulation

Five steps or requests (at least) can be made:

1. As a person included in the database, you are selected (or *de facto* qualified) for a draw and likely to be selected by this draw (the probability might be indicated).
2. Selected for a draw, you can waive this registration in the database and be removed from the list of people participating in this draw (your participation is requested, expected, but not forced).
3. You have the right to be included in the database and all you have to do is show your acceptance to be included in the base and your wish to participate in the draw (this is a declaration of acceptance, close to a passive application, with the subsequent possibility of withdrawal).
4. The population called upon to serve as the basis for the draw is limited to a certain number of people selected for this draw and then selected by this draw, and you must register as early as possible to participate (this is the version closest to a candidacy, but intermediate in intensity between a registration in an electorate and the candidacy for an election by vote).
5. By manifesting your candidacy for this draw, you agree to serve in the body selected by the draw (candidacy).

Secrecy or Transparency

This question applies mainly to the preparation of the draw, to the publicity of its result and to the conduct of functions. There are many possibilities between the practice of absolute secrecy and total public transparency. As a guarantee of transparency, a small audience made up of curious observers attend the drawing of lots. In other cases, the operation may be seen by a larger audience.

- Option: visibility. Most drawings of lots require transparency and the public eye. The base consists of a public list. This transparency protects against fraud during the preparation and practice of the lottery. Fraud during the establishment of the base is possible, and it remains possible during the draw operation. The publication of data and acts allows public control. It is logically linked to the principle of participation and publicity. It is therefore preferable to operate with a publicly visible base. You must know who is registered in the database and then who is selected by the draw.

- Option: confidentiality. Keeping a secret or a share of secrecy about a database or the outcome of a lottery is seldom necessary. This is, however, the case when the college or jury of those chosen by lot are required to work confidentially. Sometimes these chosen ones need to be protected before and after the draw, for example if they act in a dangerous context, if they are exposed to threats. Confidentiality can also be instituted because of outside influences or attempts at corruption. The procedure is no longer fully visible to remain free from interference.

When withdrawals are authorized or when individuals will eventually be unable to fulfil the functions, there are two possibilities: either having selected a number of people higher than the number of officials and to use this list as a pool, or make a new draw when the time comes. The first possibility saves time and procedure, but it hardly guarantees secrecy, since the waiting list risks filtering through the public in several places.

Withdrawal after the draw can be authorized in order to protect people who are in danger in their function or who find themselves in a conflict of interest. Threats can cause a person to withdraw against their will. If the secrecy of the drawing of lots and that of the function is ensured, then the prohibition of withdrawal seems more consistent. Protecting people and their function, guaranteeing the smooth running of work most often involves phases of visibility and confidentiality. This question arises from different angles at all stages of the procedure.

Penalties or Rewards

In these options, we try to enhance participation, distribute permissions and incentives.

- Option: penalties. Penalties are set in the event of refusal to be entered in the base or in the event of withdrawal after the draw. These fines or other legal consequences, as well as temporary ineligibility for election by vote, form a middle ground between strict obligation and absence of coercion. By comparison, voting is more active than accepting to belong to a database, but less active than accepting one's selection by lot. There are similar options regarding the compulsory or optional nature of the vote. Fines and penalties generally accompany compulsory voting. Rewards for voting are possible, although very rare in politics. Compensation or attendance fees compensate the vote in certain activities.

- Option: remuneration. Are the honour, the pleasure of participating, the interest in public affairs or the resulting self-esteem sufficient rewards as soon as citizenship is valued in a society? However, this may not be enough for several reasons: cumbersome function, difficulty of the task, momentarily annoying interference with a personal situation. Financial compensation is the most plausible positive reward. This function salary is commensurate with the scope of the task. It should not be too weak when it comes to integrating poor people. A salary significantly higher than the national or local average would harm almost no one. It can be argued that such participation should not be based on greed. The salary cannot be a big prize, but only a small one. It is justified by the compensation for the time spent performing the function and for the value it confers on it. A decent salary, for better or for worse, is one of the signs of value in our societies.

Frequency

The main options relate to the unique or renewable nature of the draw for those chosen by the lot.

- Option: non-renewable. The individuals chosen by lot are eliminated from the other draws and removed from the future base by the same procedure. If rotation in the functions is the finality, it is contradictory and counterproductive to allow to be renewed those returned to the base.

  When the selection is not renewable, the rotation is maximum. In very large databases, when the population is infinitely more numerous than the small volume of people selected by the draw, there is no point in crossing out the lists of those already selected by the draw because the probability of being selected a second times tends to zero. Renewal can nevertheless be prohibited in principle, symbolically.

- Option: renewable. When the numbers of those chosen by lot are large and the practice very collegial, the possibility of being elected twice (never more than two) is possible so that the re-elected can bring their experience to the renewed forum. The practice of an assembly of 500 or 1,000 people drawn from a base of 10,000 to 20,000 people justifies a possibility of renewal. Allowing more than two would slow down the rotation.

In small databases of 50, 100 or a few hundred, if refusal and withdrawal are authorized, authorizing unlimited renewal of registration in the database becomes economical and makes it possible to keep the interest of the greatest number. This is similar to a passive application.

These different options in various sizes attract attention to their combination. In case of refusal to be in the base or in case of withdrawal after the draw, will we be automatically eliminated from the other draws? It would be a slight penalty. Conversely, the possibility of returning to the base after refusal or withdrawal somewhat favours these reluctant behaviours since they have no impact on future rights.

Training Course

Whether or not to give training to those chosen by lot, before or after the draw, strongly depends on the degree of qualification required and the dimension of obligation.

- Option: before or after the draw. If the base has been broadened as much as possible by the qualification, the performance of certain functions will require training in some cases. The function must be carried out under the best conditions of information and training. Citizen training can be scheduled before or after the draw. It is expensive to form an entire base when its population exceeds a small volume. The other, cheaper and more targeted, option is to train only the selected ones. It remains to be seen whether such training opens the door to corruption or manipulation during their training. This necessary training can turn into oriented or distorted training. The advantage of the first costly possibility is that the selected officials are already trained and ready for the function immediately after the draw. In addition, a greater number of people in the base benefit from it. In this case, no space is left for manipulation.
- Option: without training. When there is no need for training, the situation allows immediate employment. This option contributes to the prevention of corruption and to the guarantee of impartiality. It is for this reason that the citizen juries of the courts of Athens were drawn in two stages, a first time and in large numbers to constitute a database of the Popular Tribunal for a long time, and a second time in smaller numbers to constitute a jury at the last moment, on the eve of any trial.

Chapter 7

Several Possible Uses

The examples of procedural sequences which will now be presented relate only to the use of sortition. This exploration shows which options are possible, which choices must be made among these options.

Procedural Sequence

To begin with, consider a parallel with electing by vote which includes a large number of options comparable to selecting by lot. The importance of these options varies, however, depending on whether it is a vote or a draw.

Qualification → database: yes/no.

"Yes/no" reminds us that two options are possible: proceed to a qualification (yes), not to do a qualification (no). Strictly speaking, even without any qualification restriction, it will nevertheless be necessary to define the official base for a draw as for a vote by universal suffrage. Then the qualification having given a base, this one can be used as it is or be reduced by refusals (to be registered, to remain in the base) and/or be reduced by being limited to the candidatures (when the voluntary act to participate is required). This applies to a draw as well as to a vote.

Basis → refusal (yes/no) → applications (yes/no).

This step is necessary for the drawing of lots as for the vote. There are in fact votes where any eligible candidate is considered a candidate.

Qualification → base → application → operation (vote or draw).

The operation consists of adding votes by voting or subtracting names (or numbers) by drawing:

Operation → election → withdrawal (yes/no) → nomination.

After having verified the regularity of the procedure, during a vote or a drawing of lots, a formal nomination process ends the procedure. Different withdrawal methods are possible. Leaving the possibility of withdrawing at this stage is more plausible when there has been no candidacy, whether in a ballot or a draw.

Finally, the options should be set after appointment. Either the people elected remain in the future base and will be able to participate in another draw. Or, because of their election, they are withdrawn from any subsequent base. The intermediate option comes down to giving them the choice to be registered again or not:

Appointment → re-registration in the database (yes/no).

Recapitulation of the sequence common to a draw and a vote:

Step 1: population → qualification → database for the selection (more or less smaller than the population). Latitude left or not: registration in the database is compulsory, or allows for the possibility of refusing to be registered in the database, or requires the voluntary act of application.
Step 2: base → operation (ballot or draw, addition of votes or extraction of names) → election (compiled results).
Step 3: election → withdrawal (if possible or excluded) → nomination.
Step 4: entry into office (following the voting or drawing procedures).

Complete sequence: Population → qualification → base (compulsory, or with the possibility of refusal, or with candidacy) → election → withdrawal → appointment.

These steps will be visible in the examples given in this chapter. We will add to the description several important points: the probability of being selected by the draw, the nature of the functions, the duration and the number of sessions. This brings us into a procedural area that is no longer linked to the operation or even to the draw procedure in itself.

We need a matrix as a frame for possible uses of sortition.

Base (size, volume): equal to or less in volume than the population concerned.

Subject: the body or institution drawn by lot.

Refusal (to be registered for the draw): by various means this amounts to being allowed to stay away from the base, thus avoiding participating in the future draw.

Probability of being chosen by lot: the chance of being selected by the draw in each case mentioned. Here given in order of magnitude and not to the nearest unit. The important thing is to know if it is in the order of very likely (1/2 or 1/3), or very possible (1/10), or unlikely (1/100), or very unlikely (1/1,000) and less and less likely (1/10,000 to 1/1,000,000 or more). However, this probability must be corrected upwards if the successive draws are numerous and spread out over time. If I have a 1/10 chance of being elected in an institution and I participate in 30 successive draws in a lifetime, the most improbable (although possible) is the fact of never being elected. For 50 people drawn at random out of 5,000, the chance of being elected, draw after draw, in the first draw is 1/5,000. It then increases very slightly with each draw, going from 1/9999 to 1/951 at the draw of the last person elected. What matters here is the overall probability, the chance for a person to be elected after the full draw of 50 people out of 5,000, or 50/5,000 = 1/100.

Withdrawal: possible or not after the draw.

Functions: exercised by the people chosen by lot.

Sessions: of the body designated by the drawing of lots.

Renewal: possibility to participate again in the next draw or in a subsequent draw and therefore perform the function twice.

In cases where the function is compulsory for the chosen one, it must be ensured that a majority of the people concerned have accepted the principle. For this reason (starting with this first example and for the following ones), the surest and rightest way would be to consult the population through a referendum. So, in the first example: do a majority of students agree to be submitted to a draw? A majority of favourable votes seems to be a legitimate condition for implementation. If the function is optional, before and after the draw (refusal then withdrawal both accepted), an initial positive vote would at least bode well, without being essential for the experiment.

University Bodies

We must now better understand sortition as a device, that is to say, face the realities of procedures. Let's talk about sortition for university bodies (assembly, council, committee).

Imagine a Council of 50 students chosen by lot for a one-year term
The base is a university of 5,000 students.

Refusal (to be on the list) is prohibited. Because all the students are concerned as users of the establishment and as members of an academic population.

The probability of being chosen by lot is one in a hundred (1/100).

A withdrawal is allowed after the draw or during the session but a good reason must be given. Participating in the Council is a duty as well as a right.

The functions are consultation by the administration, proposal of questions to be put on the agenda, publication of reasoned opinions, initiatives, suggestions, petitions and votes.

The discussion and deliberation sessions are public or in camera.

Renewal: several successive elections by drawing lots are authorized for an individual. The probability that a person will be chosen by lot a second time remains low. If that happened, that would be really lucky for this individual, since the total probability of being picked twice before the two draws was a one in ten thousand chance.

Another Council of 50: Academic Council of 50, gathering professors, researchers and academic equivalents

Base: 250 people, academic community of this university.

   This council is selected for a one-year term.

   Refusal: prohibited.

   Probability of being chosen by lot: one chance in five (1/5).

   Withdrawal: prohibited.

   Functions: the Academic Council of 50 has prerogatives comparable to the Council of 50 students. The fundamental difference is its effect of rotating academics. For the students, their stay is too short to involve a rotation. It would take a Council of 1,000 people at least to achieve this rotation.

   Sessions: around ten per year.

   Without any need for restriction, the law of probabilities will allow you to serve once, twice, maybe three or four times in your life if you have spent all your professional life at the same university. In this case, the probability of not having been selected is very low.

Council of 15

Base: 250 people (same base as above).

   Subject: Board of 15 members.

   This board has much work to do. This Council contributes to important decisions and their execution. Being part of it is equivalent to a part-time job.

   Refusal: Due to the burden, the procedure allows the 250 academics concerned to refuse to be on the list for the draw. This possibility of refusal may not be granted indefinitely, however, considering that academics have to accept that at one time or another this honour or chore is an obligation.

   Probability of being chosen by lot: one in sixteen chance (1/16). No strong rotation.

   Sessions: weekly.

   Withdrawal: prohibited, since refusal was authorized.

Detail: given the existence of various disciplines, it is conceivable that several parallel draws should be made and that several simultaneous draws in each department be added.

Possible adjustment: in this council of 15, half + 1 of the members are drawn (= 8/250) and the other half is chosen by a vote of the faculty (7/250). A tripartite formula is also possible: by approximate 1/3, 5 appointed (by the president of the university, the responsible ministry or other), 5 chosen by lot and 5 elected by vote.

Likewise, the most appropriate options will be chosen for other examples differing in scale, use, context, purpose.

Provided that each experiment is carefully conducted and scrutinized, it will provide much more knowledge than an endless debate over general ideas about procedures.

Local Politics

A town of 150,000 inhabitants. Two institutions: on the one hand, juries or deliberative assemblies at the level of the municipality; on the other hand, the presence of elected officials on the municipal council. Their roles, which are very different, require different degrees of qualification: a broad qualification for the juries, more restricted for the councils.

Local consultative assembly of 100

Base: no specific qualification, database identical to that of universal suffrage, all adults in possession of their civic rights.

Subject: one hundred people chosen by lot for deliberation and consultation on local political issues.

Refusal (to be registered): authorized. Two options: everyone is warned that they are likely to participate in the draw, unless they refuse to register. This is a passive version of the list. The alternative is that one must show an acceptance of being on the list. This implies that the number of registrants will be a little lower, since an act of acceptance had to be made.

Probability of being chosen by lot: this probability depends on the proportion of refusals. If one in two people agrees to participate in the draw, the probability of being elected is around 1/500 in a city of 150,000 inhabitants (the number of adults and voters being lower than the number of inhabitants).

Withdrawal: prohibited, except in the event of incapacity. Acceptance was manifested by the possibility of refusing or agreeing to be registered.

Functions and sessions: public discussion and public deliberation and behind closed doors. Consultation, deliberation, reasoned opinion.

Renewal: authorized, because the probability of renewal by the draw remains low (around 1/500).

Municipal council

The proportions are clearly restricted in the case of the council. For this, a motivation test is necessary: the application. To this must be added a quorum (minimum number of candidates before the draw) in order to guarantee sufficient participation of the population.

Subject: 10 seats out of 50 for the entire board (20%) are allocated by the draw.

Base: the qualification for the application, which allows registration in the database, is assigned by sponsorship to the candidates. These sponsorships are given by current and past members of the board and by the candidates in the present election by vote.

If you want a less socialized approach, the other option is the individual application without sponsorship. It acts as a self-qualification.

This is to avoid that the number of entries in the draw is too small. Accordingly, the process is subject to a quorum (2,000 candidates for the draw). For the 40 seats allocated by vote, as usual, there will be several lists, that is to say a hundred candidates divided into several lists. For the draw you need a higher number. A quorum ensures this by requiring, for example, that at least 2,000 people stand as candidates for election by lot. This number can be higher, it cannot be lower. This quorum thus makes it possible to exceed the volume of activists or close relatives revolving around the lists.

Refusal: impossible, they are candidates.

Probability of being chosen by lot: depending on the number of sponsored candidates. The probability of being chosen by lot will be between 1/10,000 and 1/5,000 if the will to participate is clear. It cannot fall below the quorum of 2,000 required for the base (the probability then drops to 1/2,000).

Functions: these 10 people drawn by lot in a municipal council sit among the 50 elected by ballot.

Sessions: regular and over several years (6-year mandate in France in 2017).

Disclaimer: Prohibited or limited with rare exceptions. Training could be provided to elected representatives of the draw.

Renewal: authorized. The probability of being elected twice by the lot is low.

In parallel with the regional councils.

Assemblies, councils or juries meet, generally to address different local issues. Their opinions lead to proposals subject to future legislation or to a referendum.

Provincial Politics

Advisory board or jury of 504 chosen by lot

Base: identical to universal suffrage, all adults in possession of their civic rights.

Refusal (to be registered): authorized, for lack of a positive response to the registration notification. Failure to respond serves as a refusal. In a more constrained version, without manifestation of refusal, the tacit agreement for the drawing would be recorded. This strong incentive, however, lends itself to contestation in the event of election by lot. The person concerned may declare, in good or bad faith, that they have not received any notification.

Quorum: requiring a minimum acceptance of the draw seems legitimate, between 10 and 20% of the base. For example, for 10% acceptance from a potential base of 2 million, the quorum would be 200,000 people agreeing to participate in the draw. Without this quorum, the procedure would not be continued.

Probability of being chosen by lot: in a region of several million inhabitants, assuming 500,000 acceptances, this probability is 1/1000.

Withdrawal: after the draw or during the session, it is prohibited, except in very specific conditions and in cases of incapacity.

Functions: consultation, deliberation, reasoned opinion, vote. Control of regional legislative activity, recommendations, preparation of texts.

Sessions: concerning the public debate and the internal sessions to prepare the debates, one can envisage either a series of dense and close sessions on a single subject and lasting a few weeks, or sessions spaced and spread over several months, over various objects and of longer duration.

Renewal: authorized, because unlikely, of the order of 1/1000.

National Politics

Let us imagine a tricameralism: the National Assembly, Senate, Popular Assembly form a new political system combining voting and drawing in different forms. Two hundred senators elected from the draw on the basis of one million qualified (probability = 1/5,000).

The National Assembly, at the centre of the system, is elected by a majority vote as it is today. The Senate remains an upper house and small in size. Its members are chosen by lottery after qualification by different institutions and legal organizations (civil society included). The qualified population (in the order of a million) would include people who have proven competence in their field. In doing so, the senatorial aspect (of a certain age and worth) would be retained or strengthened. A Senate of 200 people over 40, as in the example below. Finally, a People's Assembly is drawn among the entire population, on the basis of the rights to participate in universal suffrage. At least initially experimental, its operation would be limited to consultation, discussion and control.

These three extremely contrasting types testify to the very variable potential of the draw. Such a system includes three different and complementary types of representation: active and expert in the Senate, political and partisan in the National Assembly, descriptive and unprofessional in the People's Assembly.

National Assembly

Centre of the system, it is elected by vote, by majority vote by constituency or by proportional representation or even according to a mixed system including the two types of ballot. It retains the last word on legislation.

Senate of 200

Basis: the source is not universal suffrage but a smaller population, on the order of 1 to 2% of the national population. These candidates for the draw are qualified through a process of appointment by different legal institutions (elected or appointed political bodies, universities, associations, professional unions). In short, these one million people over 40 are qualified to have accomplished a work or a quality of work in their field. It is a form of call for candidates, but very broad and watered down. The instances form the basis of the draw by addition. The method of appointment is left to the qualifying bodies: hierarchical appointment, election by vote, or by drawing initially within them. Certain designation procedures are obviously excluded: sale of places in the base or any opaque and uncontrolled procedure. These designation bodies in the database choose their procedure. The regularity of this is checked from the outside.

Refusal (to be registered): authorized, at the level of each body presenting candidates (we can therefore imagine a different regime depending on these bodies: obligation or possibility of refusal).

Probability of being chosen by lot: 1/5,000.

Disclaimer: prohibited.

Functions: legislative and supervisory work typical of an upper house.

Sessions: Senate renewable by half every three years.

Renewal: authorized.

A mixed Senate in its election procedure is conceivable: half of the Senate is elected by vote, the other by drawing (2 x 100 or 2 x 150).

People's Assembly of 1,680

Base: close or equivalent to the base for universal suffrage.

Refusal (to be registered): authorized. Participation is encouraged. Registration in the database is done automatically and does not require any action. Unsubscribing requires a personal process.

Probability of being chosen by lot: depending on the acceptance rate to be registered in the database, the probability varies between orders of 1/5,000 to 1/15,000.

Withdrawal: forbidden except incapacity during the session.

Functions: questions to the government, hearing of senior officials and experts, consultative votes, right of initiative in matters of legislation.

Sessions: half of the People's Assembly is chosen by lot every two years (840/1680). This allows for the transmission of the training acquired and a time to learn internal procedures.

Operation: in addition to plenary meetings, such an Assembly can set up parallel bodies of smaller size (3 x 560; 5 x 336; 10 x 168) in order to share the work. It also gives the possibility of forming three bodies working in parallel on the same subject after an internal drawing of lots and of comparing their conclusions. In the event of disagreement, the majority of the sub-assemblies win: 2 to 1 among three assemblies of 560, 4 to 1 or 3 to 2 if it is among five assemblies of 336.

Remuneration: if the work performed corresponds to a professional half-time and if participation is actually observed, the remuneration would be around three times the minimum wage. It seems preferable that those elected to the People's Assembly keep a part-time professional activity.

If the person selected by the draw is absent from more than half of the sessions and meetings during a semester, he or she is replaced by a person coming next on the list of the drawings. This list has not been made public. The person replacing her therefore only learns of her election by drawing (old and preserved) shortly before taking office. No representative reservoir awaiting replacement is known to the public.

Renewal: authorized. The probability is tiny. It is not forbidden to simultaneously be a candidate for the National Assembly or the Senate.

European Politics

The idea of connecting, anchoring, confronting the bureaucracy of the European Union with samples, councils or assemblies of citizens remains very elusive in the prospects of the Union, according to its leaders, although such allusions are made from time to time. The forest of academic research barely conceals the European democratic desert. The European Union, by its size, could innovate at different levels: regional, national, European. All the possibilities are offered to the Union, in terms of constitution of bases, of broad or restricted qualification, of functioning by consultation, opinion or decision, on the model of the various preceding examples.

Epilogue

In many respects, the instructions for use which have just been exposed show how flexible, variable and adaptable sortition can be. Its potential contribution remains very underestimated, often caricatured negatively or positively, through peremptory judgements. However, it is these details and the pragmatic reflection on their use that will allow us to move away from prejudices and begin a programme of reflection and experimentation. The multiple possibilities offered by the draw are in themselves a call for use that strikes a balance between daring and precaution.

Any regime, any institution can use the lottery. We were particularly interested in uses consistent with democratic principles: equality, impartiality, fairness, participation, representation, freedom. This proposed use of the lottery mainly concerns democracies.

How many democratic regimes in the world in 2024? By counting large, within the limits of basic components, one can say: about one democracy for three sovereign countries. By being more demanding, we only find about thirty. In the literal sense, if the people should have the first and the last words in politics when they want it, only one state, Switzerland, is unquestionably democratic. The important thing is not in these rankings. All democratic regimes and many more or less political institutions would benefit from considering sortition as a procedure and the draw operation, testing it, evaluating it. It is only after having experienced the procedures that a first global assessment is worth being made.

May this book have helped to clarify, explain and encourage the use of one of the few procedures available for the organization and practice of democratic societies. It is your turn to enter the game.

www.ingramcontent.com/pod-product-compliance
Lightning Source LLC
Chambersburg PA
CBHW040141270326
41928CB00022B/3285